WARRIORS OF THE CLOUDS

A LOST CIVILIZATION IN THE UPPER AMAZON OF PERU ❖ KEITH MUSCUTT

PHOTOGRAPHY AND TEXT **by Keith Muscutt**

MAPS AND DRAWINGS **by Vincent R. Lee**

BIBLIOGRAPHIC ASSISTANCE **by Douglas Sharon**

UNIVERSITY OF NEW MEXICO PRESS ■ ALBUQUERQUE

Published by the University of New Mexico Press

Library of Congress Cataloging-in-Publication Data

Muscutt, Keith.
Warriors of the Clouds : a lost civilization of the upper Amazon of Peru
/   Keith Muscutt.
         p.   cm. ....
ISBN 0-8263-1962-9 (pbk.)
ISBN 0-8263-1979-3 (cl.)
1. Kuelap Site (Peru)   2. Indians of South America—Peru
—Chachapoyas (Province)—Antiquities.   3. Chachapoyas (Peru :
Province)—Antiquities.   I. Title.
F3429.1.C43M87   1998
985′.46—dc20   96-26459
                                                    CIP

Designed by Bonnie Smetts Design

Printed in Singapore by Toppan Printing Company

First Edition

MI CHUQUIBAMBA

Mi Chuquibamba, tierra querida,
La preferida y bella eres tu.
Lindos paisajes bajo tu cielo,
Bendito el suelo donde nací.

Hermosos cerros, fieles sentinelas,
Te dan tus sombras y tranquilidad.
Las suaves brisas del Chacahuayco
Frescan los campos donde crecí.

Tu gente es buena, noble y humilde,
Con su trabajo que honra te dan.
Chuquibambino, amante al trabajo,
Vamanos pronto a trabajar.

Linda es mi tierra de Chuquibamba;
En Amazonas no hay otro igual
Patron San Pedro, Patron del pueblo,
Envíanos siempre tu bendición.

Tierra querida, cuna de amores,
Eres mi ensueño y mi adoración.
Quiero a mis padres con toda el alma
Igual que a ellos te quiero a ti.

My Chuquibamba, beloved homeland,
You are the chosen and lovely one.
Beautiful is the country beneath your skies,
Blessed is the ground where I was born.

Majestic mountains, faithful sentinels,
Give you their shade and tranquility.
And the soft breezes of the Chacahuayco
Refresh the fields where I grew up.

Your people are good, noble, and humble,
And with their work they honor you.
Chuquibambinos, lovers of labor,
Let us all get to work soon.

Beautiful is my homeland, Chuquibamba;
In Amazonas, there is no equal.
Saint Peter, patron of our town,
Send us your eternal benediction.

Beloved homeland, cradle of affections,
I dream about and worship you.
I love my parents with all my heart,
And, as I love them, so I love you.

—*A ballad by Felipe Vergaray of Chuquibamba*

CONTENTS

PREFACE
6

ACKNOWLEDGMENTS
10

CHAPTER ONE
Kuelap, Citadel of the Chachapoya
13

CHAPTER TWO
Andean Civilization
23

CHAPTER THREE
Exploring Chachapoya Ruins
35

CHAPTER FOUR
Modern Communities in an Ancient Chachapoya Landscape
57

CHAPTER FIVE
Exploring the Eastern Montaña
77

CHAPTER SIX
The New Chachapoya
99

CHAPTER SEVEN
Vira Vira
103

CHAPTER EIGHT
Epilogue: The Laguna de los Cóndores
120

A CHACHAPOYA BIBLIOGRAPHY
124

PREFACE

This book is about the Chachapoya, sometimes called the Cloud People, the creators of a little-known civilization that flourished about a thousand years ago in a remote region of the upper Amazon, within the boundaries of the modern nation of Peru. It is also about the people who now inhabit the same region: some descendants of indigenous people, some descendants of their European conquerors, and most descendants of both.

In 1973, I decided to see the world. Like many of my contemporaries, I was disillusioned with my own civilization and needed some perspective. I wanted to live life for a while without possessions, visit monuments to the genius of other civilizations, and experience the "alternative realities" of other cultures.

To accomplish this it was necessary for me to study a map of the world, stick colored pins in all the places that were sufficiently exotic, and then decide on the logical order in which to visit them. As I plotted what I imagined would be my uniquely personal odyssey, countless other equally restless and disaffected souls were sticking colored pins in the same places on their own maps, for essentially the same reasons. Thus I inadvertently braided my destiny into the meandering itinerary, known as the "hippie ant-trail," that wound its way from the United States through Mexico and Central America, heading inexorably toward Peru and the crown jewel of ancient American ruins: Machu Picchu.

The places along this route were magnificent, but something indispensable was missing: try as I might, I could never make more than superficial contact with the local people. They recognized me for what I was—a member of the vagabond horde of that era, a backpacking *jipi* who had come to visit not them but the relics they happened to live near; a bird of passage, another here-today, gone-tomorrow gringo.

By the time I reached Machu Picchu and beheld the superlative masonry and panoramic vistas, I felt like an intruder. Instead of experiencing the fulfillment I had anticipated, I was overwhelmed by a loneliness as primal as stone and as infinite as the Andean landscape. I had arrived at the apogee of spectacle and the nadir of intimacy simultaneously.

Before leaving the United States, in one of those latent epiphanies that subsequently change the trajectory of a life, I had been introduced to Juan-Tomás Rehbock, an Argentinian adventurer. Juan-Tomás showed me his slides of the "lost city" of Gran Pajatén, which had recently been rediscovered in the rain forests of the upper Amazon. Its mysteriously evocative, jungle-shrouded ruins immediately captured my imagination, though at the time they seemed far too inaccessible for me to visit.

But now they beckoned me. A protracted visit to a remote place like that, I supposed, might enable me to escape my stereotype and establish a personal rapport with the local people. Back in Peru's capital, Lima, I found a book, *Antisuyo,* by Gene Savoy, a North American explorer and journalist who, among many other salutary accomplishments, had become the first outsider to publish photographs of Gran Pajatén. In *Antisuyo,* Savoy surveyed the ruins of the ancient civilization of the Chachapoya, to which Gran Pajatén apparently belonged. Further research on my part turned up explorer Victor W. von Hagen's earlier book, *Highway of the Sun,* where he described his Inca Highway expedition, which took him into Chachapoya territory. Both authors made it clear that the area was rarely visited and poorly explored, and that the people of the region were friendly to outsiders. My mind was made up.

A few weeks later, after a grueling journey by bus, truck, mule, and foot, I was living in a log cabin in the department of Amazonas, deep in ancient Chachapoya territory. As the guest of Mónica and Eleuterio Cisneros, I sampled life on the brink of subsistence and the frontier of the "civilized" world. Mónica and Eleuterio had taken me in like a long-lost son. Every evening they regaled me, in their singsong dialect, with their personal biographies, which they embellished with anecdotes about magical encounters with the spirits that inhabited the limestone caverns and pre-Columbian ruins nearby.

Their neighbors insisted that I visit them, too, and share their hospitality and information. When I repaired a broken radio, I became useful, and the news spread. Soon people were trekking to the village with antiquated machinery for me to fix in exchange for food, with which I replenished my hosts' larder. I slept under the stars, to avoid being parasitized by the fleas that infested their household animals, but had to keep my toes covered so they did not become hemoglobin spigots for the vampire bats that plagued the anemic cattle. By day, I hiked vibrantly colorful, fragrant trails to plentiful Chachapoya ruins and explored caves strewn with bones and with pottery shattered by fallen stalactites. I was enamored of the people and incurably addicted to exploration.

I have subsequently, to paraphrase Thoreau, traveled much in Amazonas. I have discovered, to my frequent discomfort, why so few outsiders go there—and, to my constant delight, why many more should. In studying the remains of the Chachapoya civilization, I have developed a profound respect for its remarkable accomplishments. And I have come to appreciate that the descendants of the Chachapoya, although materially impoverished, are among the wealthiest people in the world when honesty, generosity, humor, and compassion are considered riches. From both the ancient and the modern Chachapoya I have learned what I set out to discover: that civilization is community.

A WORD ABOUT WORDS

In writing this book, I attempted to strike a balance between accuracy and brevity. To provide a context for the ancient Chachapoya it was necessary for me to synthesize, with far less definition of terms and detailed discussion than the subject merits, a great deal of information about Andean prehistory, much of it still fragmentary and controversial.

Moreover, the field of cultural history is subject to intense debates that are continuously changing its vocabulary. For instance, giving dates with reference to the Christian calendar or using such terms as *pre-Columbian* raises ethical questions. I do not want to diminish the importance of such debates, even though some might be dismissed as truly academic, because others force us to be objective and alert to bias. However, doing justice to these intellectual issues can make prose indigestible. Therefore, I have assumed that readers are capable of creating culturally sensitive definitions of commonly understood terms without my belaboring them with circumlocutory or condescending language, which is offensive in its own way.

Words I had particular difficulty with were, predictably, *discovery, city, civilization,* and the like. Discovery is completely relative, of course. From the point of view of the readers of *National Geographic,* Hiram Bingham undoubtedly discovered Machu Picchu. From the point of view of others, however, including an earlier visitor who had written his name in charcoal on its walls, not to mention the family who lived in the ruin and guided Bingham through it, knowledge of Machu Picchu's existence would hardly have come as a surprise. It would be dishonest of me to pretend that I don't like to "discover" things that, from my own point of view, have been unknown; but the things I "discover" almost invariably are familiar to local people and have already been seen by earlier travelers who simply left no record of their passing. As for the term *city,* very few population centers in ancient Peru, and none in the Chachapoya region, fit any reasonable definition of this word. But the terms *town* and *village* fail to capture the essence of Chachapoya hilltop communities; hence my choice of the word *citadel,* which, fortunately, has the blessing of several reputable archaeologists. Similarly, the words *civilization, culture, society, ethnicity, polity, state, empire,* and so on, imply different things to different audiences. I have used them loosely and somewhat interchangeably, in part to avoid tedious repetition.

Peruvian place names are also quite troublesome. The names of communities are subject to change, and spellings vary. (For instance, Pusak may be spelled Pusac, and Cajamarquilla was formerly spelled *Caxamarquilla* but then changed its name to Bolívar.) Some names are generic and reappear in a host of different places (for instance, Yanayacu, meaning "black water"). Adding to the confusion is the Peruvian custom of calling a section of a river by the name of a nearby community. To simplify matters, I have referred to the main course of a river by the same name throughout its length, although, since the exact source is not always known to me, even this practice could lead to confusion. Ruins, too, have many different local names, many of them quite mundane, and explorers are prone to glamorize their alleged discoveries by giving them more inspiring designations.

Consequently, plenty of sites were never really lost; they were simply mislaid or misfiled. A sizable number have been "discovered" more than once (notably Gran Pajatén, which, amusingly, was even *re*-discovered and made sensational "Lost City in the Andes" headlines on an otherwise dull day in the news during 1985). My guiding principle in citing place names has simply been to report whatever I thought would be least confusing to the reader or most likely to be found on a map or in a bibliography. I regret that the confines of this book have not allowed for more, and more detailed, maps, although I think the reader will find Vincent Lee's maps the most lucid ever produced that deal with the Chachapoya. I have listed a few useful maps in this volume's bibliography, compiled with the assistance of Douglas Sharon; many of the books and articles listed there also contain maps. Handheld global positioning system satellite-navigation devices will soon be obligatory equipment for archaeological exploration, and I look forward to the day when an inventory of Chachapoya sites will collate their various names and spellings and all the published references to them, keyed to their geographical coordinates.

Finally, the academic world is in the process of evaluating the way in which words in the Inka (note this spelling) tongue should be transcribed in our alphabet. For instance, *Wari* and *Tiwanaku* have replaced *Huari* and *Tiahuanaco* in most of the recent literature, and *Kuelap* has supplanted *Quélap*, *Cuélap*, and several other alternate spellings. I have generally gravitated toward recent conventions, believing that a few years from now the substitution of *Inka* for *Inca* will be no more an affront to the eye than the substitution of *Beijing* for *Peking*. I have retained a few of the older transcriptions, however—for instance, in the personal names of the Inka leaders. And I have not added English plural, possessive, and adjectival suffixes to Quechua words, so what might have been *Incas*, *Inca's*, *Incas'*, and *Incan* have all become simply *Inka*. I now write "the Chachapoya" but hold no grudge against anyone accustomed to calling these people "the Chachapoyas." It hardly seems worth arguing about whether to add an "s" to the end of the Spanish corruption of a garbled Inka name for a people whose name or names for themselves, in their own language, we do not know.

ACKNOWLEDGMENTS

Many people contributed directly or indirectly to this book. I would like to acknowledge them.

For their guidance in the field and on the printed page, thanks to Pelayo and Amelia Jáuregui Zamora and their family and to Abel Vega Ocampo, Douglas Sharon, and Vincent and Nancy Lee. I am heavily indebted to the scholars whose names appear in the text and bibliography, especially Inge Schjellerup, whose knowledge of the Chachapoya is boundless, and Federico Kauffmann Doig, Warren Church, Peter Lerche, Waldemar Espinoza Soriano, John Hemming, and other academic authorities on the Chachapoya. I would like to thank Juan-Tomás Rehbock for contributing the photograph that appears on page 76. Thanks are similarly due to many independent researchers, explorers, naturalists, journalists, and photographers—in particular, Adriana von Hagen, Victor W. von Hagen, Gene Savoy, and Morgan Davis. I also wish to thank Carlos Torres Más, Director of the Instituto Nacional de Cultura, Filial Amazonas, for permitting me to visit and photograph the archaeological remains within his jurisdiction. Harry Crosby, author and explorer of Baja California, set an example to which I aspired, and master photographer Al Weber refined my vision.

Eleuterio Cisneros Grandez, the late Mónica Melendez, and other inhabitants of Caserío Mito gave generously of what little they had before I even knew how to ask for it. I could never adequately express my gratitude to the people of Pusak, Chuquibamba, Uchucmarca, and neighboring communities, especially Felipe, Leilde, and Gilmer Vergaray; Nicolás, Angel, and Selis Jáuregui; Zoila Abanto; Narsario Zamora; Zenaida Silva; Narciso Carrión; Alejandro Silva; Serbio Silva; Calixto Bardales; Luis Adán Portal; Felix Portal; Julio Camán; Francisco Adalisio; Julián Contreras; Adolfo Contrino; Milcíades Rojas; Abundio Valle; Pedro Silva; Rómulo Ocampo; Wilington Jáuregui; Neli Ponce; and the *madres* of the Convento Patmos. Thanks to the Gregorios Sánchez, father and son, creators of the Museo Regional del Marañón, and to Daniel Quirós, all three of Celendín. My gratitude to the people of Leimebamba, Atuén, and La Morada who blazed the trails and showed me their discoveries, especially the pioneering Añazcos, Benigno, Gregorio, Zacarías, Fabian, Eyner, Táusen, Miguel, Senilser, and their families; Nilo Díaz; Santos Sicha; Custodio Rengifo; my *compadres* Segundo and Lucrecia Bardales and their family; Dr. Alfredo Abarca Salazar; Vassily and Jesús Goñas; and countless others who provided me with information and hospitality. I can only hope I have remembered (and spelled) their names correctly.

Thanks to my traveling companions over the years, Justine Vacco, John "Scott" Anderson, Katherine Butler, Dr. Clyde Byfield, Doug McVay, and Jennifer Peck; to personal friends and collaborators John Ammirati, the late Peter Reyner Banham, Tandy Beal, Mike Brod, David Cope, Del Cover, Lyndy Dean, Diane Gifford-Gonzalez, Lol Halsey, Ken Hedges, Phil Hofstetter, Herman Jesson, Doug and Marge McClellan, Mike Marx, Elanie Moore, Patti Moore, Juan-Tomás Rehbock, Audrey Stanley, Su Suttle, Christina Waters, and Kate Wheeler; and to many others who encouraged me, reviewed manuscripts, and generally tolerated—or exacerbated—my Chachapoya addiction.

My professional colleagues at the University of California, Santa Cruz, have been exceptionally generous in accommodating my involvement in this project, and I am proportionately grateful to them. Many thanks to Rita Bottoms, Curator of Special Collections at the University Library at UCSC, whose energy and networking skills connected me with Pomegranate Artbooks, and to UCSC Cartographic Librarian Stan Stevens.

I salute Don Montague, founder of the South American Explorers Club, who keeps it all in perspective, and tip my hat to Gina Gertberg of The Travel Spot for smiling, instead of grimacing, whenever she saw me coming. On behalf of the parents and children of Chuquibamba, many thanks to friends in the United States who have given generously to the Fundación Benéfica Niños de Chuquibamba, and thanks also to Mac Holbert and Graham Nash, who supplied Amazonas with enough guitar strings to fill its air with music for years to come. Long-deferred gratitude goes to David Burdett, who predicted that I would never write this book, thereby provoking me to do so. Abundant thanks to the alchemists at Pomegranate Artbooks who first transmuted my sow's ear into this silk purse: Thomas and Katie Burke, Jill Anderson, Xavier Callahan, and Bonnie Smetts; to Beth Hadas and her team at UNM Press; and to David Wagg for making the necessary connections.

Finally, I would like to acknowledge my constant indebtedness to my mother, Mary Muscutt, and to my late father, George Muscutt, who got me started in more ways than one. With the possible exception of my parents', any errors are exclusively my own.

CHAPTER ONE

Kuelap, Citadel of the Chachapoya

In 1843, seventy years before Hiram Bingham broadcast the splendor of the Inka "lost city" of Machu Picchu through the pages of *National Geographic*, Juan Crisóstomo Nieto, in an obscure letter to a regional administrator, proclaimed the discovery of Kuelap, a colossal ruin hidden in the rain forests of the Amazonian Andes. Whereas Machu Picchu was immediately catapulted into international fame, Kuelap was never widely publicized, and it languishes in relative obscurity. Like most explorers, Crisóstomo Nieto exaggerated the size of his find, but Kuelap is nevertheless a truly magnificent monument to the skill and industry of pre-Columbian people. It is ample testimony that the Inka were not the only ancient Andean civilization to build on a megalithic scale.

Kuelap, usually described as a fortress, although "citadel" would be a more apt description, occupies a mountainous ridge at an elevation of about 9,500 feet above sea level, in the headwaters of the Amazon. The nucleus of the site is seven hundred yards long, averages a hundred yards in width, and covers about fifteen acres. It is surrounded by a massive perimeter wall with three narrow, shaftlike entrances. One flank of the citadel stretches along the rim of a steep cliff. The remainder of the citadel is protected by about eight hundred yards of sheer wall ranging in height from thirty-five feet, where the ground rises, to over fifty, where it dips. This wall is precisely engineered, with thirty or more level courses of finely cut and fitted limestone blocks, each weighing up to three tons. Despite (or perhaps because of) its enormity, it blends harmoniously with the rolling landscape, across which it undulates like a gargantuan stone anaconda.

Inside the perimeter wall (actually the façade of an artificial terrace) are the ruins of over four hundred stone buildings, almost all circular, ranging from about ten to thirty feet in diameter. Most of the buildings have collapsed or have been demolished down to their foundations; a few remain standing as high as twelve feet. Assuming that they were originally capped with conical thatched roofs, they would have reached an impressive height. Each has a single doorway. These buildings, presumably dwellings, are

Kuelap. Kuelap's main portal, one of three entrances that penetrate its outer wall. Today, a solitary custodian is Kuelap's only permanent inhabitant.

Kuelap. The crumbling façade of Kuelap's perimeter stretches almost half a mile across the landscape. Over four hundred circular buildings, arranged in clusters and linked by passages and stairways, fill the interior.

Kuelap. Admission to Kuelap was architecturally controlled. Entrances are narrow, tapering passageways, and only one person at a time can filter past the final checkpoint.

scattered in rows and clusters and fill the enclosure like rafts of bubbles. There is little semblance of overall planning, yet the buildings exhibit a pleasingly organic relationship with one another and with the natural and artificial contours of the terrain. A second interior terrace is contained by another massive, finely crafted wall, some thirty-five feet high and reminiscent of the inner keep of a medieval European castle. This enclosure, called Pueblo Alto, is more spaciously organized. Its buildings, some of which are rectangular, open on a plaza; this arrangement suggests that the enclosure was a ceremonial precinct.

One extremity of Kuelap is dominated by an *atalaya*, a solid rectangular tower that apparently served as a lookout post as well as a bastion from which to defend the population against attack from along the mountain ridge. The principal monument at the opposite end of the site is an extraordinary building, nicknamed the Tintero because its inverted conical form, with sides flaring outward as they rise, resembles an old-fashioned inkwell. The interior of the Tintero is a bottle-shaped, corbeled vault. The neck of the vault forms a chimney that can be entered from above. Until recently, the Tintero was believed to have been a depository of ritual offerings, or perhaps a mausoleum. Not long ago, however, James McGraw, a member of a survey team from the San Diego Museum of Man, noticed that the chimney is not vertical but deliberately tilted. Preliminary measurements indicate that the sun at noon on the day of the winter solstice, a pivotal day in Andean ritual and agricultural cycles, shines down the chimney and projects a beam of light into the interior. On the floor of the Tintero lies an engraved slab of rock—dislodged, unfortunately, by treasure seekers—that may once have served to track the movement of the sun. The Tintero was perhaps a solar calendrical observatory.

Many of the structures in Kuelap seem to have served ceremonial or funerary functions. Even the perimeter wall incorporates burials, fragments of which can still be seen through cracks in the masonry. Archaeologist Alfredo Narváez, after counting over a hundred interments, concluded that "in reality the outer wall is a cemetery." Kuelap is now littered with human bones exhumed and scattered by looters; the modern custodian of the site takes a ghoulish delight in decorating niches in the buildings with discarded skulls.

Who built Kuelap when, and why? These questions are largely unanswered. The architects of this ancient citadel were members of a group of regional cultures collectively referred to as the Chachapoya. Archaeological research, which is scant, shows that Kuelap was occupied from about A.D. 800 to 1500. The earlier of these dates may indicate that Kuelap was originally conceived as the centerpiece of an effort by the Chachapoya to defend themselves against the expansion of the Wari cultural empire, which exerted control over much of the central highlands and coast of Peru around that time. If so, this effort was successful, because there is little if any evidence of Wari influence at Kuelap.

Kuelap. Only the foundations of most of the round buildings remain. This one, a ceremonial structure, has a geometric frieze overhung by a protective cornice, a signature of Chachapoya architecture. The significance of the rhomboidal design is unknown. It may symbolize either snake or jaguar, both of which were deities in the Chachapoya pantheon.

We know from historical sources that by A.D. 1500 the Inka empire had conquered the Chachapoya, and there are many fragments of Inka pottery at Kuelap to confirm the arrival of the Inka. An account of their hard-fought battles with the Chachapoya during the late fifteenth century, transcribed from Blas Valera's lost manuscript by the chronicler Garcilaso de la Vega, does not include Kuelap in the list of fortresses and villages subdued by the Inka. Kuelap lies roughly between Suta and Levanto, the last two important Chachapoya communities that Garcilaso says were conquered, and Suta and Levanto offered only token resistance when they saw that most of the Chachapoya territory was already in Inka hands. Perhaps the Inka simply bypassed Kuelap, and it later surrendered without a fight after all the neighboring communities had capitulated, when further resistance would have been futile. Nevertheless, Alfredo Narváez's excavations produced an arsenal of 2,500 slingshot missiles cached on top of Kuelap's defensive tower, so its occupants were certainly prepared for battle at some point in their history. It is hard to imagine that the Chachapoya simply gave up their most imposing citadel without a struggle. One suspects that Garcilaso's informants did not know—or perhaps tell—the whole story.

The Spanish conquest of the Chachapoya, which commenced in 1535, was complicated and protracted, but Kuelap was not, so far as we know, the scene of battle. There are few references to Kuelap after the advent of the Spanish. In 1538, the rebellious Manco Inka, advised by Chachapoya allies, set out to make a fortress near Levanto his refuge during his struggle to regain native independence from the Spanish. The historian John Hemming believes that this fortress was Kuelap, but I am inclined to think that Manco was seeking a more isolated, less conspicuous refuge, probably in the forests farther east. In any event, Manco's Chachapoya allies in the area were defeated, so Manco abandoned

Kuelap. Early travelers reported numerous sculptures in Kuelap. This one, embedded in the Tintero, is one of the few that remain.

the project and set up his government-in-exile at Vilcabamba instead. In 1572, according to archives studied by the Peruvian historian Waldemar Espinoza, the remaining population of Kuelap was forced out and relocated in less defensible towns, or *reducciónes*, established by the Spanish. The buildings were torn down, but their foundations and the perimeter walls defied destruction. Parts of Kuelap were later reconstructed, rather shabbily, and reoccupied. By the seventeenth century Kuelap, like Machu Picchu, had simply disappeared from the consciousness of everyone except the few families who continued to live in its immediate vicinity and took it for granted.

It is a humbling experience to stand beneath the towering walls of Kuelap and try to imagine the staggering investment of energy consumed in its construction. Estimates of the total volume of material that was transported to build it are unreliable, but Kuelap is undeniably one of the most massive monuments of the ancient Americas. Radiant in the warm glow of the morning sun, it still makes a powerful declaration of the might of its builders, and of the scope of their imagination.

Kuelap today remains much the same as it must have been when Juan Crisóstomo Nieto and his *macheteros* hacked their way into it a century and a half ago. A few trails and structures are kept clear for visitors, but exuberant rain-forest vegetation has reclaimed the interior of the site. Over the centuries, the round ruined roofless buildings have been transformed into giant flowerpots for trees laden with mosses, vines, orchids, and bromeliads. From an outlying fortification higher up the ridge, Kuelap is barely visible under its mottled green canopy of vegetation. If a ruin as enormous as Kuelap can be so easily camouflaged in this landscape, how many lesser ruins, one wonders, remain undetected?

Kuelap. Human remains excavated by tomb robbers now litter Kuelap.

Kuelap. An arboreal orchid blossoms in Kuelap's verdant canopy.

Kuelap. Kuelap's trails, except for a few kept open for visitors, are choked with cloud forest vegetation, as are Kuelap's masonry towers and labyrinths.

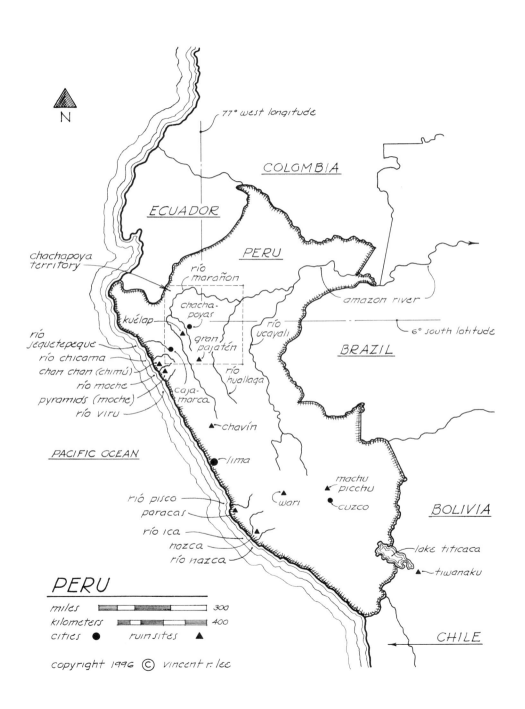

N

77° west longitude

COLOMBIA

ECUADOR

PERU

chachapoya
territory

río
marañon

chacha-
poyas

amazon river

kuélap

río ucayali

6° south latitude

río
jequetepeque

gran
pajatén

río chicama

chan chan (chimú)

río huallaga

BRAZIL

río moche

caja-
marca

pyramids (moche)

río viru

chavín

PACIFIC OCEAN

lima

machu
picchu

río pisco

wari

BOLIVIA

paracas

cuzco

río ica

nazca

río nazca

lake titicaca

tiwanaku

PERU

miles   300

kilometers   400

cities ●   ruin sites ▲

CHILE

copyright 1996 © vincent r. lee

CHAPTER TWO

Andean Civilization

The Chachapoya was one of many civilizations that evolved in the New World in complete isolation from the Old World civilizations of Africa, Asia, and Europe. It flourished for several centuries before the European invasion of Peru and left many impressive monuments to Chachapoya genius. Yet, surprisingly, the Chachapoya people have been largely neglected by archaeologists and historians. Textbooks of pre-Columbian history mention them only in passing, if at all, perhaps because Chachapoya civilization arose in a remote and rugged region, where there are many obstacles to scientific archaeology. Or perhaps it is because the destruction of the Chachapoya cultural heritage was, for reasons that we will explore, so sudden and complete that we can only speculate about the Chachapoya way of life. And, to a large degree, it is because Peru is so well endowed with archaeological remains that there is simply not enough money and expertise to study and conserve more than a fraction of its rich cultural heritage. In any event, the role played by the Chachapoya in the prehistory of the Andes is very poorly understood.

By far the best-known ancient civilization of Peru is the Inka. The later stages of Chachapoya civilization coincided with the rise of the Inka, with whom the Chachapoya were in protracted conflict. All the ancient civilizations of Peru lacked certain vital technologies of the Old World, such as the wheel, iron, and explosives, but they excelled in many aspects of the arts and sciences. By the time of the Inka, they had also developed social structures and communication systems capable of governing ethnically diverse and far-flung populations. These structures and systems were aided by a method of record keeping somewhat analogous to writing: the *khipu*, a bundle of colored and knotted cords that served primarily to tally numbers and was also used as a memory aid in the transmission of other types of information. At the time of the Spanish invasion and conquest of South America, the Inka had deployed their administrative skills to annex the vast and varied territories that today comprise the modern nations of Peru, Ecuador, Bolivia, and Chile, territories encompassing an area approximately equal to that of the Roman empire. The Chachapoya were one of the ethnic groups eventually incorporated into the Inka empire. Had the European invasion occurred two or three centuries earlier, however, the conquistadores would have encountered a very different situation. At that time, the Inka would have been a minor power and the

Chachapoya a comparatively major one among the many different cultures thriving in Peru, all of them the descendants of a long sequence of advanced civilizations that had risen and fallen over preceding millennia.

THE NATURAL ENVIRONMENT AND PREHISTORIC CULTURES OF PERU

Peru has an astonishingly rich and varied cultural history. Geographically, it provides many differing environments for human habitation, often abruptly separated by natural barriers. These habitats have been occupied by ethnic groups that developed distinct cultural adaptations. Some of the habitats were exploited as long as 10,000 years ago by nomadic hunters and foragers, whose ancestors had crossed from Asia into the Americas when Ice Age conditions lowered sea levels and united the two continents. Each of the four main subdivisions of the natural environment—the Pacific coast, the coastal deserts, the Andean highlands, and the Amazon basin—gave rise to distinct cultures.

Before they developed agriculture, domesticated animals, or learned to fire ceramics, people began to settle the Peruvian coast, exploiting its exceptionally rich fisheries and leaving stone tools, household debris, and burials to testify to their existence. As early as 4,000 years ago, coastal dwellers were cultivating cotton and employing a large repertoire of visual symbols. Increasing dependency on agriculture, however, was drawing populations away from the coast and into the fertile valleys. With the introduction of edible crops, including squash, chili peppers, and beans, but still before the invention of pottery, huge ceremonial mounds involving the movement of tens of thousands of tons of material were being constructed a few miles inland.

Between Peru's coast and the Andes is a narrow strip of rainless but foggy coastal desert segmented by numerous rivers that drain the western slopes of the Andes to the Pacific. The valleys of these rivers and their immediate surroundings became the home of many cultures that were fundamentally similar but evolved with considerable individuality, since they were isolated from each other by stretches of inhospitable desert. Maize (corn), peanuts, and various tubers were added to the crops under cultivation. Ceramic vessels, invaluable for holding water and for cooking and storing grain, first appeared between 3,800 and 3,500 years ago. In addition to mastering the art of firing ceramics, these cultures wove intricate textiles on heddle looms. They also worked copper, silver, and gold with amazing technical skill and artistry. As their populations swelled, they devised ambitious systems of irrigation in order to expand the area under cultivation. The growth of craft specializations, as well as the construction, maintenance, and governance of networks of canals, necessitated complex forms of social organization and governance that were reflected in increasingly elaborate ritual activity. These valley civilizations of the coastal desert built with *adobe* (mud brick), often on a massive scale. Their leaders were buried with sumptuous offerings of ceramics, textiles, shell, precious stones, and metal artifacts. Among the cultures that developed in and around Peru's desert valleys were the Paracas, weavers of rich textiles; the Nazca, famous for their enigmatic ground markings; the pyramid-building Moche; and the successors of the Moche, the Chimú, architects of the sprawling metropolis of Chan Chan.

The Andes, a series of parallel, north-to-south–trending mountain ranges, or cordilleras, are the geological backbone of Peru. The Andean cordilleras are separated from one another by deep intermontane valleys that generally drain toward the north and the east, flowing via the Marañón, Huallaga, and Ucayali Rivers into the Amazon. The Andes are second only to the Himalayas in elevation, with numerous peaks exceeding 21,000 feet in Peru and in neighboring Bolivia, Chile, and Ecuador. Between the snowline and the timberline are windswept grasslands variously referred to as *puna, pajonal, jalca,* and *páramo* according to their degree of coldness and wetness. In the southern Peruvian Andes, at an elevation of 12,500 feet, is Lake Titicaca, a freshwater sea surrounded by a vast treeless plain, the *altiplano.*

In all these highland environments, too, beginning some 4,000 years ago, diverse civilizations sprang up in relative isolation from one another. The best-known ones are those that eventually exercised widespread cultural influence or military power: the Chavín, the Wari, the Tiwanaku, and the Inka. But there was also a long succession of less influential or less aggressive highland cultures, one of which was the Chachapoya. All were heavily dependent on the cultivation of frost-resistant tubers, especially potatoes, and such grains as quinoa, which thrives at higher elevations. Maize, squash, and beans were farmed at lower elevations. Llamas were domesticated for food and wool and for use as cargo animals. *Cuy* (guinea pig) supplemented the diet. Many of these highland cultures produced superlative masonry and were capable of quarrying, transporting, dressing, and tightly fitting granite blocks weighing over a hundred tons.

On the eastern slopes of the Andes, in the *oriente,* lie the steep rain forests of the *montaña,* which gradually blend into the seemingly infinite lowland Amazon jungle, or *selva.* An important subdivision of the *montaña* environment is the *ceja de la montaña*—literally, the eyebrow of the *montaña.* The *ceja* is an atmospherically turbulent region with abundant rainfall caused by warm, moisture-laden air welling up from the Amazon basin and encountering cold air masses that descend from the high Andes. In the equatorial latitudes of northern Peru, pockets of cloud forests can be found at elevations exceeding 12,000 feet. Conversely, although some might be surprised to hear of them, there are Amazon deserts, arid zones where rain falls on one side of a mountain range and leaves the opposite side in a dry "rain shadow." These varied environments are sharply delineated by formidable ridges and canyons.

The inhabitants of the *oriente* are usually called *tribes* and stereotyped by the primitive connotations of that word, but they, too, developed rich and complex societies. The names of these cultures and the languages they spoke are innumerable. Their distribution across the landscape and across time is so dynamic and convoluted as to be practically indecipherable. Some of these were cultures of nomadic hunters and foragers. Others were of seminomadic farmers who cut down and burned swaths of forest, planted, and moved on when weed infestation and deterioration of the soil reduced yields. Still others formed villages beside rivers and lakes.

Agricultural tribes grew various crops, especially *yuca* (manioc) and the prized narcotic coca, which they traded to their highland neighbors. Given the lack of imperishable materials (such as stone)

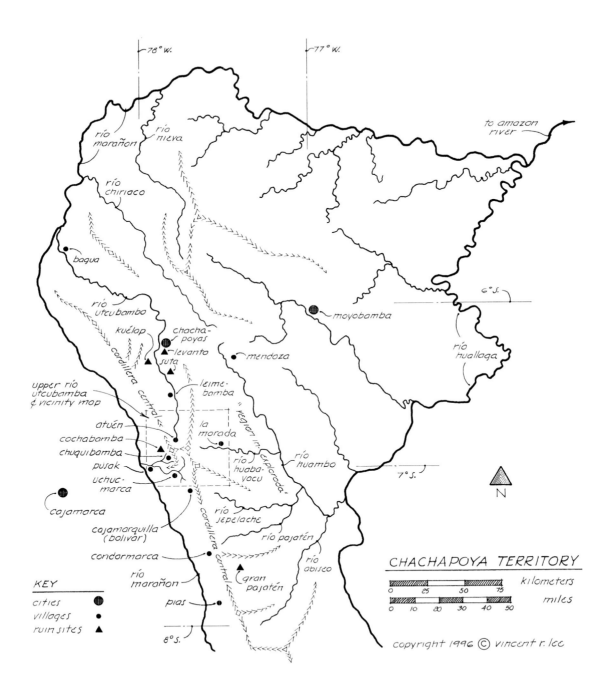

to amazon river

78° W.

77° W.

río marañon

río nieva

río chiriaco

bagua

6° S.

río utcubamba

moyobamba

kuélap

chacha-
poyas

río huallaga

levanto
suta

mendoza

upper río
utcubamba
& vicinity map

leime-
bamba

cordillera central

"region inexplorada"

atuén

la morada

cochabamba

chuquibamba

río
huaba-
yacu

río huambo

7° S.

pusak

uchuc-
marca

N

cajamarca

río
jepelache

cajamarquilla
(bolivar)

río pajatén

condarmarca

río
abiseo

cordillera central

CHACHAPOYA TERRITORY

río
marañon

gran
pajatén

kilometers

KEY

0   25   50   75

cities

miles

villages

pias

0   10   20   30   40   50

ruin sites

8° S.

copyright 1996 © vincent r. lee

and the rapidity with which jungle environments rot or wash away archaeological remains, very little evidence of ancient rain-forest cultures has been preserved. Nevertheless, it is becoming increasingly apparent to archaeologists that the inhabitants of the *oriente*, far from being culturally retarded, provided many of the foundations on which the highland and coastal civilizations were based. Ceramics made their appearance in the Amazon basin earlier than elsewhere in Peru, and many of the earliest cultivars of the Pacific coast are of jungle origin.

THE CHACHAPOYA TERRITORY AND ORIGINS

In this cultural and geographical quilt, the Chachapoya civilization occupied a roughly trapezoidal patch of territory in northern Peru, a prolongation of the Central Cordillera of the Andes, bounded by the Marañón to both the west and the north and by the Huallaga to the east, between five and a half and eight degrees south of the equator. The short, southern boundary of this trapezoid is where the Marañón and the Huallaga, which drain opposite sides of the Central Cordillera, come to within a hundred miles of each other. The longer northern boundary is less well defined but runs roughly between the modern towns of Bagua and Moyobamba. The total surface area is about 25,000 square miles.

The Marañón is Peru's westernmost major Amazon tributary. Its northward course keeps it close to the Pacific for its first 250 miles, but then it sweeps around toward the east, where it slices through the Andes. A hundred miles farther east, the Huallaga, another voluminous river system, joins the Marañón from the south. Together, they skirt the northern tip of an eastern range and

embark on a meandering 3,000-mile journey through the lowlands of the Amazon basin to the Atlantic. The environment in the area bounded by the Marañón and the Huallaga ranges from torrid jungle in the lowlands to frigid treeless highlands around the 15,500-foot summit of the Nevado de Cajamarquilla, with desert, *ceja,* and *jalca* sandwiched in between. Here is how Garcilaso de la Vega characterized the verticality of the terrain: "The natural difficulty of the countryside is so rugged that on some roads the Indians slide down ropes a distance of eight or ten times the height of a man, for there is no other way of advancing."

The passes through the Andes that take advantage of the canyon of the Marañón are the lowest for hundred of miles in either direction. Therefore, they were important avenues of migration and trade between the Amazon basin and the coast. Excavations at archaeological sites along this route have shown that commerce among the coastal, highland, and jungle cultures was well established at least 3,000 years ago. In the centuries that followed, ephemeral and poorly studied cultures infiltrated and settled the land between the Huallaga and the Marañón. One of these must have been the rootstock of the Chachapoya civilization. Fragments of the Chachapoya language that have been preserved in place names hint that the Chachapoya may have spoken a dialect of Carib, which would indicate that they had entered the area via the Amazon basin rather than from the Pacific coast or highlands.

Chachapoya civilization, typified by its uniform and distinctive architecture, probably coalesced around A.D. 800, when construction at Kuelap began. Between A.D. 800 and the second half of the fifteenth century, the era of the Inka invasion, the

Chachapoya cleared and terraced hillsides and built their characteristic stone citadels throughout the region. The scale, distribution, and defensibility of Chachapoya settlements suggests that they were relatively independent polities—a confederacy of *ayllu* (clan groupings) engaged in shifting alliances and internecine conflict rather than components of a persistent monolithic state. They may have been capable of uniting to defend themselves against external threats (perhaps the Wari), as suggested by the sheer enormity of Kuelap; nevertheless, their response to the Inka, several centuries later, was poorly coordinated, indicating the lack of cohesion among these clan groupings. In the period between the decline of the Wari and the rise of the Inka, people throughout the highlands abandoned large, urbanized population centers and scattered into fortified hilltop settlements, apparently as the result of a centrifugal dispersion of power after the collapse of the Wari center of gravity. The size and distribution of Chachapoya communities fit comfortably into this larger Andean settlement pattern. At the height of their civilization, the Chachapoya may have numbered over a quarter of a million, dispersed among hundreds of communities ranging in size from a few families to a thousand or more inhabitants.

THE INKA CONQUEST OF THE CHACHAPOYA

The beginning of the end of Chachapoya civilization was the Inka invasion, which occurred around A.D. 1475. Inka society is often romantically portrayed as a pre-Columbian Utopia, and it is certainly true that Inka rule brought many advantages with it, not the least of which was the orderly production, storage, and distribution of food and the resulting insurance against famine. But the Inka state was also a totalitarian, dynastic theocracy that expanded its power primarily through the threat or use of force. It was a warfare state as much as a welfare state. Like the imperial Romans, to whom they are frequently and justifiably compared, the Inka embodied the noblest aspirations of humanity while practicing its cruelest atrocities. Consequently, the Inka were fiercely resisted by the Chachapoya.

Although the defeat of the Chachapoya by the Inka ruler Túpac Yupanqui was swift, the Chachapoya rebelled repeatedly against his successors Huayna Cápac and Huascar. For this they were severely punished. Chachapoya warriors were executed en masse. As much as half the remaining population was deported to other parts of the Inka empire, and colonists from elsewhere, or *mitmaqkuna* were brought in as part of an Inka program of ethnic dispersion. The remains of an administrative center that the Inka built to control the Chachapoya can still be seen at Cochabamba. Other Inka administrative outposts and military garrisons are found throughout Chachapoya territory. In fact, the name *Chachapoya* is a Hispanicization of the name given to them by the Inka in their Quechua or, more properly, Runasimi, tongue. Its meaning is disputed, but its derivation from *Sacha Puya*—roughly, "Cloud People"—if not correct, would certainly be apt. We do not know how the Chachapoya referred to themselves in their own tongue or even if they considered themselves to be a single people.

THE INKA CIVIL WAR

No sooner was Inka dominion over the Chachapoya consolidated than a disastrous civil war broke out. The Inka ruler Huayna Cápac apparently died suddenly of smallpox, which was sweeping through South America in advance of the Spanish themselves, who had introduced it into indigenous populations. The chaos in the Inka court caused by the epidemic and by Huayna Cápac's sudden demise resulted in a war of succession.

The empire had been unwisely divided by Huayna Cápac between two of his heirs. A southern, Cuzco-based portion, which included the Chachapoya, was assigned to Huascar. A northern, Quito-based portion was assigned to Atahualpa. Predictably, Huascar and Atahualpa were soon at war with each other. The Chachapoya were caught, geographically and politically, in the crossfire of this conflict. Some Chachapoya sided with Atahualpa; others were conscripted to Huascar's losing cause and suffered heavy casualties, including 7,000 warriors lost in a single battle. This massacre turned the Chachapoya population decisively against the ultimately victorious Atahualpa, and after the Chachapoya taunted and skirmished with Atahualpan auxiliaries on the banks of the Marañón, Atahualpa exacted vengeance. He mounted a punitive expedition into Chachapoya territory, executed Chachapoya leaders, and ordered all adolescents of both sexes deported.

Cochabamba. An Inka building in Cochabamba serves as a cattle pen.

THE SPANISH CONQUEST OF THE INKA AND THE CHACHAPOYA

The arrival of Spanish conquistadores, which coincided with the victory of Atahualpa over Huascar, was greeted by the Chachapoya and other Inka vassals as an opportunity to cast off the Inka yoke. When the Spanish captured Atahualpa at Cajamarca, in 1532, Chachapoya leaders promptly presented themselves to Francisco Pizarro and pledged allegiance to him. Pizarro's conquest of Peru was following the template of Hernán Cortés's conquest of Mexico, where ethnic groups resisting oppressive Aztec domination had quickly allied themselves with the Spanish invaders.

The benefits of the Chachapoya affiliation with the conquistadores were only temporary, however. In effect, by helping the Spanish defeat the Inka, the Chachapoya had cosigned their own death warrant. Some Chachapoya warriors did eventually fight alongside Inka troops and distinguish themselves in the epic battle for control of Cuzco, but their fate was already sealed. The Spanish, by defeating the Inka, also assumed sovereignty over the Inka vassals and swiftly replaced the despotic Inka regime with their own.

The first Spanish incursion into Chachapoya territory was a brief reconnaissance led by the conquistador Hernando de Soto in 1532. Soto was dispatched by Pizarro to investigate a rumor of Inka-led warriors massing in Levanto to attack the Spanish, who were then holding the Inka leader Atahualpa for ransom in Cajamarca. Soto penetrated as far as the Utcubamba but found no evidence of the rumored offensive.

Shortly after Hernando de Soto's return, Guamán, a Chachapoya leader who had acted as an Inka proxy ruler in Cochabamba, arrived in Cajamarca to pledge allegiance to the Spaniards. Perhaps Soto had persuaded Guamán to join forces with the Spanish to overthrow the Inka regime. Guamán had immediate and pressing motives to seek an alliance with the Spanish: despite the capture of Atahualpa, Inka forces were still in power and were enforcing Atahualpa's punitive order to deport all male and female adolescents of Guamán's clan. In any event, Pizarro already knew enough about Guamán to welcome and greet him by name when he presented himself in Cajamarca.

After receiving much of the ransom they had demanded for Atahualpa's freedom, the Spanish treacherously garroted him. Next, they conquered the Inka capital of Cuzco; installed Manco Inka, one of Huascar's descendants, as the titular head of state; and sent Spanish troops to sack and garrison the provinces of the disintegrating Inka empire. In 1535, Alonso de Alvarado occupied Cochabamba with a force of four horsemen and three infantrymen. Guamán not only acquiesced to but also assisted in this invasion. Alvarado probed Chachapoya territory as far north as Levanto. Meanwhile, Guamán pillaged Cochabamba and the surrounding communities. He accumulated a chest full of gold and two chests

Cochabamba. The village of Cochabamba is built on the ruins of the administrative center established by the Inka to consolidate their conquest of the Chachapoya in the late 1470s.

full of silver (treasures that had somehow escaped becoming part of Atahualpa's ransom) and handed them over to Alvarado. The Chachapoya, or at least those under Guamán's control, were too weakened by decades of conflict with the Inka, and too confused in their allegiances, to prevent even this tiny handful of the seemingly invincible foreigners from extorting from them what little they had left. By this time, Guamán must have recognized the scope of the Spanish threat to the Chachapoya, but, apparently practicing the politics of expediency, he shrewdly preserved whatever wealth and power he had accrued under the Inka by becoming a Spanish proxy instead. Alvarado, ironically, yet predictably, used his booty to recruit and arm reinforcements. A few months later, he returned with a second, larger expedition to consolidate his position in Cochabamba.

In 1536, however, Alvarado's conquest of the Chachapoya was abruptly interrupted. His help was urgently needed to put down Manco Inka's rebellion. Manco Inka was a "puppet" who had initially collaborated with the Spanish but, after enduring much betrayal and abuse, had decided to conspire against them. He orchestrated the first widespread indigenous revolt. Manco tenaciously besieged the Spanish garrison in Cuzco and sent allies to attack the Spanish headquarters in Lima. Alvarado was initially summoned to help relieve Lima and then was assigned to relieve Cuzco. In the process of fulfilling these missions, he became embroiled in civil strife, which, exacerbated by Manco's scheming, cleaved the Spanish leadership. As a result of this convoluted situation, Manco's rebellion failed and he retreated deep into the Vilcabamba jungle (from where he continued to foment rebellion throughout Peru), and the internal conflict among the Spanish was militarily resolved (by the victory of Pizarro over his archrival, Diego de Almagro). Alvarado was free—and well prepared to resume his conquest of the Chachapoya.

Even as Alonso de Alvarado was returning to Cochabamba, a contingent of Chachapoya in the vicinity of Cajamarquilla was incited by Manco Inka's emissary, Cayo Tópac, to rise up in support of Manco. This regional manifestation of Manco's rebellion was put down by Guamán's faction of Chachapoya warriors, who remained steadfastly loyal to the Spanish cause. The rebel leaders and Cayo Tópac were captured and burned alive in Cochabamba. The eagerness of one group of Chachapoya to fight and kill members of another, especially under these circumstances, provides strong circumstantial evidence for long-standing internal divisions among them.

In 1538, Alonso de Alvarado reached Cochabamba with his third expedition, which consisted of about 250 experienced soldiers. Once again, he was favorably received by Guamán. Alvarado proceeded to establish the Spanish colony of San Juan de la Frontera de los Chachapoyas, which, after two relocations, became the nucleus of the modern city of Chachapoyas. During the next decade, despite frequent popular uprisings, the colonists tightened their stranglehold on the Chachapoya. The *coup de grace* was apparently the arrival in 1547 of an army of 500 rapacious soldiers under the command of Gomez de Alvarado. Guamán, who can be characterized as either an unprincipled opportunist or a brilliant pragmatist, died in 1551. He was the last indigenous Chachapoya leader of any importance.

With the advent of the ruthlessly exploitative feudal Spanish overlords, and with the continuing ravages of contagious diseases introduced from the Old World, the Chachapoya population was decimated. Simultaneously, Spanish religious authorities were pursuing their policy of "extirpation of idolatry," eradicating native beliefs and practices throughout Peru. Thus drew to a close the final, tragic chapters of Chachapoya civilization. In less than a century, a catastrophic sequence of disasters had decimated its population and devastated its culture. Any traces of the Chachapoya heritage that may still exist, other than the ruins of their architecture, are as likely to be found in the places to which many of the Chachapoya were exiled as in their original homeland.

Cochabamba. The foundations of the church at Cochabamba are reassembled Inka stonework. U-shaped grooves perhaps evidence the Inka technique of bonding masonry by pouring molten copper into channels passing from stone to stone.

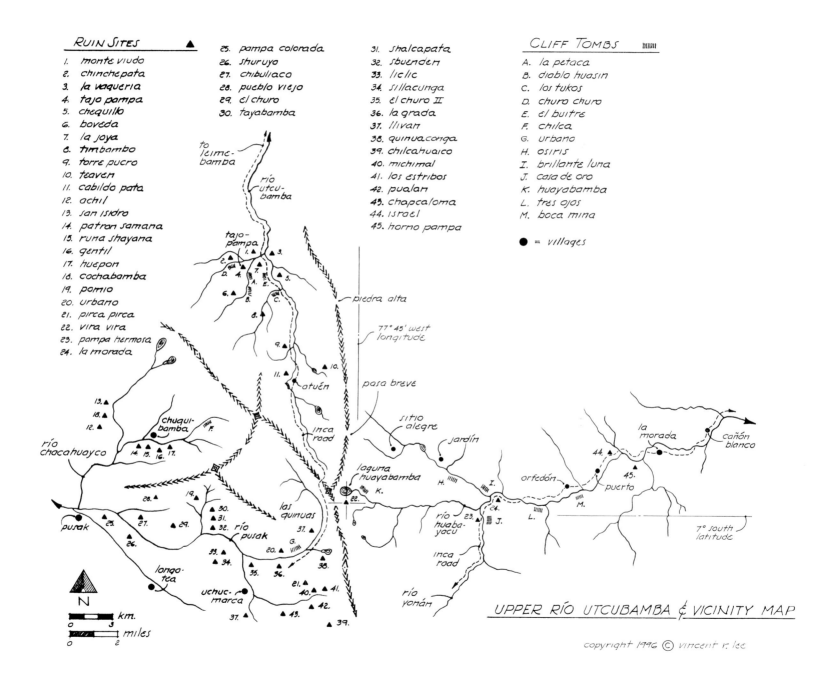

RUIN SITES ▲

1. monte viudo
2. chinchepata
3. la vaqueria
4. tajo pampa
5. chequillo
6. boveda
7. la joya
8. timbambo
9. torre pucro
10. teaven
11. cabildo pata
12. achil
13. san isidro
14. patron samana
15. runa shayana
16. gentil
17. huepon
18. cochabamba
19. pomio
20. urbano
21. pirca pirca
22. vira vira
23. pampa hermosa
24. la morada

25. pampa colorada
26. shuruyo
27. chibuliaco
28. pueblo viejo
29. el churo
30. tayabamba

31. shalcapata
32. sbuenden
33. liclic
34. sillacunga
35. el churo II
36. la grada
37. llivan
38. quinuaconga
39. chilcahuaico
40. michimal
41. los estribos
42. pualan
43. chapcaloma
44. israel
45. horno pampa

CLIFF TOMBS

A. la petaca
B. diablo huasin
C. los tukos
D. chura churo
E. el buitre
F. chilca
G. urbano
H. osiris
I. brillante luna
J. casa de oro
K. huayabamba
L. tres ojos
M. boca mina

● = villages

to leime-
bamba

río
utcu-
bamba

tajo-
pampa

piedra alta

77° 45' west
longitude

pasa breve

atuén

inca
road

sitio
alegre

jardín

la morada

cañón
blanco

río
chacahuoyco

chuqui-
bamba

laguna
huayabamba

orfedón

puerto

pusak

las
quinuas

río
pusak

río
huaba-
yacu

7° south
latitude

longo-
tea

uchuc-
marca

inca
road

río
yonán

N

km.
0   3

miles
0   2

UPPER RÍO UTCUBAMBA & VICINITY MAP

copyright 1996 © vincent r. lee

Exploring Chachapoya Ruins

Kuelap is a typical Chachapoya site. It occupies a defensible, high-altitude ridge and is built on terraces retained by stone walls. Within the retaining walls are clusters of predominantly circular buildings, a few of which are embellished with overhanging cornices that protect bands of geometric designs. The surrounding hillsides were terraced for agriculture, and sheltered ledges in nearby cliffs were used as mortuaries. The architecture is austere, with a strong tendency toward bilateral symmetry, and ceramics tend to be plain or to display only rudimentary geometric designs similar to those on the buildings. Permutations of these features are found at over a hundred known Chachapoya settlements in the modern Peruvian departments of Amazonas, La Libertad, and San Martín.

It is extremely unlikely that another ruin of the magnitude of Kuelap will be discovered. Nevertheless, because many important sites undoubtedly remain unreported, Chachapoya territory is one of a rapidly diminishing number of places in the world where one can still find ancient remains that have rarely if ever been seen by outsiders.

THE RIO UTCUBAMBA SITES

The Utcubamba is a tributary of the Marañón that bisects the mountainous Chachapoya heartland, flowing northward and passing beneath Kuelap before joining the Marañón. Many quintessential Chachapoya sites in addition to Kuelap are found in and around the Utcubamba drainage, especially near its headwaters.

My personal interest in this specific region was a result, like many other things in Peru, of serendipity. In 1981, while buying expedition supplies in the street market of Chachapoyas, I was approached by a stranger, Nicolás Jáuregui, who invited me to his home and asked me to help him repair a camera that he had been given. As I tried unsuccessfully to get the corroded shutter unstuck, I told him I was heading north to look for Chachapoya remains in a mountainous region that had never been surveyed.

Over a meal of *yuca* with *cuy*, Nicolás described impressive ruins on and around land owned by his family. (Naturally, these ruins were in exactly the opposite direction from my planned itinerary.) The inhabitants of Chachapoyas sometimes have fertile imaginations and are apt to tell listeners what they think the listener wants to hear. Descriptions of ruins, for example, often turn out to be hearsay or wild exaggerations, so at first I was skeptical. But Nicolás, a retired schoolteacher, seemed genuine and unusually knowledgeable. Furthermore, he was willing, indeed anxious, to take me to his ruins.

In Peru, one rapidly learns, a personal connection is worth a thousand plans, so a few days later I found myself, along with fellow adventurer John "Scott" Anderson, camped at Tajopampa, sixty miles south of our intended destination. There we enjoyed the hospitality of Nicolás's brother, Pelayo Jáuregui, who fortuitously had arrived the same day. Pelayo was to become my perennial mentor, guide, and infinitely tolerant companion in the pursuit of Chachapoya ruins.

We had ridden, yanked, and prodded recalcitrant mules up the trail that leaves Leimebamba, the closest town accessible by road, and follows the Utcubamba upstream. *Leimebamba* is a corruption of *Raimi Pampa*, the name imposed on one of the Chachapoya communities that, according to Garcilaso de la Vega, the Inka Túpac Yupanqui had vanquished. We were evidently ascending the ancient trail used by Túpac Yupanqui in his conquest of the Chachapoya, a trail later improved to meet the exacting road-building standards of the Inka empire. Since its improvement, however, it had deteriorated badly. In places, our mules wallowed

in mud up to their bellies while thorny *uña de gato* brambles clawed at our saturated clothing. Resplendent blue morpho butterflies swooped nonchalantly across our path, as if to mock our bedraggled appearance and labored progress.

We arrived exhausted at Tajopampa and pitched our tents on a grassy plateau above the San Miguel de Malpaso, a small tributary of the Utcubamba, just as the fleeting twilight of the tropics metamorphosed into the incomparably star-studded night sky of the Andes. Cold and saddle sore, but with pains attenuated by a generous nightcap of Pelayo's 100-proof *aguardiente*, I slept until the morning sun turned our tent into a sweat lodge.

When I emerged, I saw that we were camped below an almost vertical 1,500-foot cliff. I recognized it as La Petaca, the site of extraordinary cliff tombs first reported by Henry and Paule Reichlen in 1950 and expertly photographed in the 1960s by Gene Savoy. Exercising a modicum of journalistic license, Savoy had described La Petaca as a "necropolis," a city of the dead, and grandiloquently dubbed the ruins in the vicinity "The Cities of the Condors." As if to confirm the identification, several condors soared obligingly overhead.

Nicolás and Pelayo's deserted stone and rammed-earth farmhouse stood beside the remains of a dozen or more circular Chachapoya foundations, some of which had grindstones three feet in diameter, called *batanes*, with cylindrical rocker stones called *chungos* inside them. Decorated *chungos* had been recycled to support the pillars

La Joya is in urgent need of protection because, unfortunately, cattle are being allowed to trample it, and the circular buildings, one by one, are being cleared and converted into ready-walled potato patches. At the edge of the ruins is the home of Luis Adán Portal, a spry eighty-year-old who guided Gene Savoy. The foundation of Adán's home is made of Chachapoya building blocks. *Cabezas clavas*, stone sculptures retrieved from the ruins, adorn his kitchen and patio. As he guided us around La Joya, he told us of the night when he heard gunshots—"Pling! Pling!"—from Savoy's expedition camp. The following day, he found bloodstained rags in the ashes of the campfire. This mysteriously unexplained event still excites endless speculation among local inhabitants.

From La Joya one can see similar ruins that occupy all the nearby ridges and pampas—Monte Viudo, La Vaquería, Bóveda, Enaven (Chinchipata), Chequillo, and many more. Monte Viudo, a thickly forested ruin, is well preserved and provides tantalizing glimpses of mosaic friezes beneath a tangled mat of mossy vines. It is a prime candidate for conservation and study. A less overgrown sector of Monte Viudo is crowned by an unusual round building that sports two adjacent doorways (one with its lintel intact), a decorative geometric frieze, and a small *cabeza clava* tenoned into the wall. The highest point of Monte Viudo was evidently reserved for a ceremonial building, a feature seen at many Chachapoya sites.

La Vaquería is a ruined community of both rectangular and circular buildings. It runs for two or three hundred yards along a ridge directly across the Utcubamba from La Joya. While sheltering from

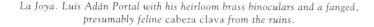
La Joya. Luis Adán Portal with his heirloom brass binoculars and a fanged, presumably feline cabeza clava from the ruins.

La Joya. The swollen cheeks and euphoric expression of this cabeza clava recovered from the ruins portray a coquero, or coca-leaf chewer.

a violent hailstorm at La Vaquería, I unexpectedly came upon a *cabeza clava* set into the interior wall of an ancient round house and had the eerie sensation of being scrutinized by a stone face whose fixed expression had remained unreciprocated for half a millennium.

Bóveda's masonry is generally more coarse than that of nearby sites and gives the impression that Bóveda is an older community, although it might just as easily be a later, decadent one, or simply one built with a poorer quality of stone. Its principal monument is a low rectangular platform with rounded corners that supports twin circular buildings.

Enaven, or Chinchipata, sits on a promontory at the confluence of the Tingo (that is, the Tinku) and the Churo Churo. It incorporates at least a hundred well-crafted, tightly packed buildings staggered up the slopes, with scalloped infills between tangent buildings, some of which have tongue-shaped additions resembling front porches. Opposite Enaven, above the Churo Churo, is a cluster of cliff tombs, barely perceptible because of the degree to which they blend in with the eroded rock face.

Chequillo, a short distance up the Utcubamba, is presumably Choquillo, the "city in the forest" first reported by Victor W. von Hagen during his Inca Highway Expedition, which anticipated Savoy's forays into the upper Utcubamba by a decade.

If all these sites around La Joya were occupied simultaneously, as may well have been the case, they must have presented a spectacular panorama of graceful white stone buildings with verdant terraces cascading down the slopes beneath them.

Farther up the Utcubamba are other ruined communities and fortifications. Timbambo, quite close to La Joya, was recently equated with Papamarca by the Danish archaeologist and ethnographer Inge Schjellerup. Papamarca is the only vanquished Chachapoya village listed by Garcilaso de la Vega that does not have a modern community with a closely corresponding name. There is no shortage of sites that might have been Papamarca, but Timbambo is a promising contender. It certainly matches the clues contained in its name: *papa* (potato in Quechua and Spanish), or possibly *pampa* (in Quechua, a flat place), plus *marka* (in Quechua, a high place or communal land). It is indeed a high, flat place surrounded by terraced fields where potatoes were probably grown. Papamarca is unusual in that one component of the ruin is situated on a slope, whereas another portion lies in a depression that has a stream running through it. The site is nestled in a valley that is naturally concealed and, to judge from the degree to which the land was modified for agriculture, exceptionally fertile. In every direction, ancient roads can be seen leading to and from Timbambo. A *lindero,* or boundary wall, runs straight across the valley through the ruins, at right angles to the stream. It ascends the slopes on both sides of the Timbambo Valley, with little regard for the natural contours of the terrain, continues over the ridges, and crosses the neighboring San Miguel de Malpaso Valley. This *lindero* is an enigmatic feature that has never been studied or surveyed. If the traces of it I have seen are any indication, it may have stretched all the way from the Marañón to the crest of the Central Cordillera. Local tradition says it was the dividing line between the Cuzco and Quito portions of the Inka empire, but it is actually too far south for that. A slightly more plausible explanation is that it defined the northern and southern Inka

La Vaquería. The round houses of La Vaquería are strung like beads along a seemingly inhospitable ridge.

La Vaquería. Dodging a hailstorm, I came face to face with this cabeza clava set into the wall of one of La Vaquería's buildings.

Monte Viudo. Well-preserved buildings with zigzag friezes are hidden in a forested summit.

Monte Viudo. A ceremonial building with two adjacent doorways, adorned with a geometric mosaic and an eroded cabeza clava, crowns an exposed prominence.

hunos (divisions) of the Chachapoya colony. This demarcation line existed somewhere between Condormarca and Papamarca, according to historian Waldemar Espinoza. In either case, it is strange that a territorial boundary would ignore the features of the landscape, so it may have had some other practical purpose or symbolic significance.

Around Timbambo are several satellite communities and fortifications, such as Chanchillo, Cruz Pata, and Torre Pukro. The latter is an imposing fortress that was visited by Victor W. von Hagen. It overlooks the terraced valley of the Teaven, a tributary of the Utcubamba bordered by an ancient trail leading to the eastern *montaña*. The Chachapoya evidently felt it imperative to monitor access to and from the *montaña* and to control the vitally important route along the Utcubamba. If Timbambo is indeed Papamarca, then Torre Pukro must have played an important role in the battle for it.

THE CLIFF TOMBS OF THE UPPER UTCUBAMBA

The cliffs of La Petaca and their continuation at Diablo Huasi, above and to the east of the San Miguel de Malpaso, are the sites of some of the most remarkable archaeological remains anywhere in the Americas. Chachapoya architects and engineers somehow contrived to scale these vertiginous walls of crumbling limestone and construct substantial and elaborate buildings on seemingly inaccessible ledges. In many instances, they even built cantilevered platforms, driving wooden poles into crevices in the rock and creating balconies on which they assembled stone sepulchers. It is almost impossible to imagine how a preindustrial society, using only fiber ropes and wooden scaffolds, without even (as far as is known) the assistance of pulleys, was able to quarry and accurately manipulate huge stones in such precipitous locations. Incredibly, these tombs have survived at least five hundred years, in some cases perhaps a thousand years, of exposure to the elements, as well as occasional earth tremors. I have spent days, indeed weeks, scanning these cliffs with binoculars, waiting for favorable conditions for photography, and have never once tired of studying them. Each inspection brings fresh discoveries. Bathed in the golden late-afternoon sun, La Petaca is one of the most spectacular and archaeologically compelling visions imaginable.

Many of La Petaca's tombs were daubed with red paint, the color associated with death in the symbolism of most indigenous American cultures. Some tombs were plastered and painted with alternating bands of red and white. Others were framed with red arches or rectangles. In many cases, the surrounding rock face was splattered with random masses of red paint—a wildly energetic action-painting effect, in stark contrast to the controlled lines of the constructions. A splash of red paint is often all that remains to mark the former location of a fallen structure. In some places, the pigment is ochrous; in others, it is so intensely vermilion that it appears to have been cinnabar, a compound of mercury so revered by indigenous people that they overpainted gold funerary offerings with it.

Figurative paintings are quite rare in Chachapoya territory, but La Petaca has one prominent and quite macabre panel. From across the canyon, two approximately life-size figures are visible on the

Bóveda. Bóveda features conical sinkholes, collapsed limestone caverns that have been sculpted into concentric terraces for agriculture— miniature versions of the well-known Inka site at Moray, near Cuzco.

Timbambo. The outlines of dozens of buildings in the lower sector are clearly visible from the upper sector of the site, as are ridged fields and roads. This sector occupies a gently sloping valley with a stream flowing through it (lower left). A lindero, presumably a territorial division, cuts through the site (diagonally across the bottom right-hand portion of the photo).

cliff face. One of the two figures wears a headdress of antlers and is clutching something that resembles a broom. The other has what appear to be rays emanating from between its shoulders. Together, these two figures depict a familiar motif in Peruvian iconography: trophy head-hunting. The "rays" are the victim's blood, spurting from its headless neck, and the "broom" is actually the decapitated head, dripping blood. A third, smaller figure and what appears to be a feathered shield adorn a projecting surface that can be seen only from an oblique angle.

There can be no doubt that most, probably all, of the buildings at La Petaca were tombs. Some of them, as can be seen from a distance, still contain mummified human remains. A few are strewn with bones tossed aside by *huaqueros*, the treasure hunters who have been busy here since the arrival of the Spanish. It is not uncommon to find bones, pottery, textiles, basketry, and cordage at the foot of the cliffs among piles of debris from fallen crypts.

In general, the human remains indicate that the Chachapoya were of large stature by comparison with most other Andean peoples. Some tombs contain a single individual. Others were used for multiple burials, possibly of families or high-status individuals whose attendants were sacrificed to accompany them into the next world. To prevent putrefaction, corpses were eviscerated and then dried and wrapped, usually in the fetal position, in textile bundles. Many of the skulls show fractures—battle wounds, perhaps, or marks of sacrificial execution. In a surprisingly large percentage of the skulls, the surgical operation known as trepanning, in which a hole is cut through the cranium, has been performed, but the reason for trepanning is unknown. The surgery may have been practiced to alleviate pressure from blows to the head. Perhaps it

was more ritual or magical in nature. There is evidence of healing in some cases, but many patients—or victims—did not survive.

The practice of mummification goes even farther back in time in Peru than it does in Egypt. Bodies have been excavated that were deliberately preserved in salt on the central coast of Peru over six thousand years ago. On the coast of Chile, near the Peruvian border, the Chinchorro mastered the art of mummification about four thousand years ago. Like the ancient Egyptians, the Peruvian cultures sent their dead into the afterlife with the textiles, pottery, tools, food, animals, and even human companions they would need with them. Mummies were stored in caves, in freestanding funerary monuments known as *chullpas*, or in underground chambers, and were periodically brought out and paraded for ceremonies of adoration. I have noticed that many of the cliff tombs in Chachapoya territory have causeways and platforms attached to them. These may have served not only for access but also as stages for ritual display of the mummies, perhaps so that the mummy bundles could be aired in the sun but sheltered during the rains. In the changeable climate of the region, display of mummies might have been a seasonal activity. There are highly polished hand- and toeholds on the routes to the tombs, confirming that the tombs were frequently revisited. The mummies of the Inka nobility—and, presumably, leaders of other cultures, too—were treated as if they were still alive. They kept their possessions, collected tribute, and were ministered to by priests and courtiers. Indeed, one motive for imperial expansion may have been that dynastic heirs had to conquer new territories because the wealth from the old estates still accrued to mummified ancestors' courts.

La Petaca. Several hundred feet of towering cliffs are honeycombed with innumerable caves and ledges where the Chachapoya erected tombs for their dead.

La Petaca. Shimmering light, caused by atmospheric thermals, frustrates extreme telephoto coverage of the cliff tombs. Even with optimal equipment, repeated visits and hours of patient observation are needed to catch the right illumination with still air. But time spent contemplating La Petaca is never wasted.

Diablo Huasi. A short distance up the San Miguel de Malpaso from La Petaca is another concentration of tombs, at Diablo Huasi (literally, Devil House). The unique demands of every natural ledge or cave not only force each building to be distinct but also offer its architects and engineers an artistic challenge. The variety of funerary buildings in the cliffs of La Petaca and Diablo Huasi contrasts with the uniformity of the surface buildings of La Joya.

Diablo Huasi. This dense concentration of tombs is in a vertical cleft at Diablo Huasi. Most of the tombs are decorated with characteristic rectangular T- or inverted T-shaped niches. These features may have had practical as well as decorative origins, serving to reduce the mass of the structures and to provide ventilation.

Diablo Huasi. Great skill and industry were required to quarry and maneuver slabs weighing hundreds of pounds in locations such as these. These achievements are no less awe-inspiring than the efforts required to erect colossal masonry on the relatively level surfaces of Kuelap.

La Petaca. In this head-hunter pictograph, the head of the victim is suspended from a cord in the hand of the victor.

The exact relationship between the Chachapoya and the tombs at La Petaca is not firmly established. Some of the tombs may belong to a separate culture, Revash, which apparently coexisted with the Chachapoya culture from approximately A.D. 1200 until the time of the Inka conquest. Revash ceramics, which are quite distinct from Chachapoya ceramics, have been excavated in and around cliff tombs at Santo Tomás de Quillay, between La Petaca and Kuelap, and some of the tombs at La Petaca resemble the Revash tombs at Santo Tomás. Other tombs at La Petaca seem more typically Chachapoya in origin, although their predominantly rectangular form is at odds with the generally circular Chachapoya surface architecture. Their decorative masonry, too, although similar, is not identical. Perhaps the spatial limitations of the rock ledges and artificial balconies dictated the rectangular shape of the tombs. Differences in decoration might also be explained by the symbolic significance of specific motifs. Morgan Davis has pointed out that Chachapoya citadels are frequently paired with Revash tomb complexes—an observation that, in the absence of archaeological studies, compounds the mystery of the relationship between the two cultures.

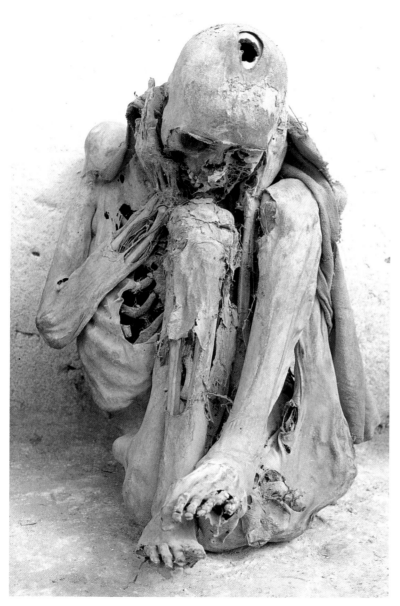

Mummy. This remarkable mummy, now in the Museo Regional del Marañón, reportedly came from La Petaca. The skull has been trepanned. The patient evidently did not survive the operation, since the scalp never healed.

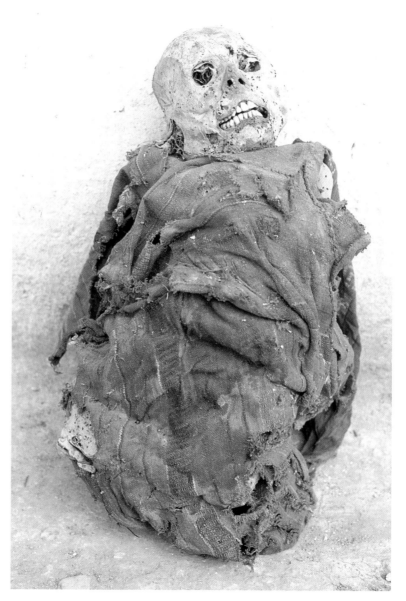

Mummy. This mummy, still wrapped in a bundle of patterned textiles, has teeth that are in far better condition than those of the majority of the area's modern inhabitants.

CHAPTER FOUR

Modern Communities in an Ancient Chachapoya Landscape

The Pusak and Chacahuayco Rivers are eastern tributaries of the Marañón that come together at the modern town of Pusak. Their sources are close to each other and also close to the source of the Utcubamba. In ancient times, numerous communities along the Pusak, Chacahuayco, and Utcubamba were interconnected by a web of roads running over the ridges that separated them.

The market town of Pusak, in the sweltering valley of the Marañón, is the modern gateway to what was once the southwestern quadrant of ancient Chachapoya territory. Until recently, the dirt road to the coast, which has no fewer than 680 switchback curves in its zigzag, 3,500-foot ascent out of the Marañón valley, ended rather summarily at Pusak. This road has since been extended as far as Cajamarquilla (Bolívar).

CHUQUIBAMBA AND UCHUCMARCA

Half a day's mule ride from Pusak are the twin towns of Chuquibamba and Uchucmarca, up the Chacahuayco and Pusak valleys, respectively. Chuquibamba and Uchucmarca are both classic Spanish colonial pueblos—flatland settlements laid out as rectangular grids emanating from central plazas. Into such communities—the *reducciónes*—Chachapoya populations were forcibly relocated from their ancient villages, whose ruins still punctuate the ridges and slopes of the surrounding mountains.

The siting of these ancient settlements at elevations higher than those occupied by today's population may have been intended to defend against both human and microscopic enemies. One of these, *uta*, or leishmaniasis, a lethal insect-borne skin infection

Pusak. Although it resembles a medieval European village, Pusak came into being only in the 1960s, when the road to Cajamarquilla was halted for lack of funds. Chuquibamba and Uchucmarca are in the cloud-shrouded highlands beyond Pusak.

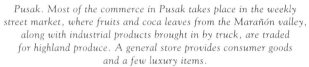

Pusak. Most of the commerce in Pusak takes place in the weekly street market, where fruits and coca leaves from the Marañón valley, along with industrial products brought in by truck, are traded for highland produce. A general store provides consumer goods and a few luxury items.

Pusak. An overshot waterwheel powers a trapiche, *which crushes juice out of sugarcane. Some of the juice will be reduced to* chancaca, *solid blocks of brown sugar, but most will be converted to alcohol and distilled into* aguardiente.

Pusak. Using a minimal but versatile technology that has not changed in over three thousand years, except that sheep's wool has replaced llama and alpaca wool, a woman weaves fabric on a backstrap loom.

Pusak. Lower elevations in the Marañón valley lie in the rain shadow of the Andes and are arid except where they are irrigated by the rivers. Outsiders are surprised to see deserts populated with thorny plants and cacti, remarkably similar to those of northern Mexico or the southwestern United States, covering large portions of the upper Amazon drainages.

that eats away the cartilage of the face, especially the lips and nose, is endemic at the lower elevations. Plagues of *uta* afflicted both native and Spanish inhabitants of the *reducciónes* and feature prominently in the folklore of both Chuquibamba and Uchucmarca. They exemplify the tragedies that occur whenever outsiders ignore the accumulated wisdom and experience of indigenous populations and summarily impose foreign customs.

Chuquibamba has served as my base of operations since the early 1980s. No vehicular road leads to it, and its only links to the outside world are a tortuous mule trail and a single frail strand of telegraph wire. Attempts to provide it with hydroelectric power have succumbed to what I suspect must have been Atahualpa's final curse—that machinery will inevitably fail in Peru. Industry and entropy are locked in mortal combat in Chuquibamba as new walls rise, Phoenixlike, from the mud mounds to which the earlier ones degenerated. The inhabitants are mestizos, of mixed Spanish and Indian descent, and although Spanish is the only language now spoken, it is laced with words and expressions from the Quechua lexicon as well as with names even more deeply rooted in the lost Chachapoya tongue.

Chuquibamba's population consists of a privileged minority, who own endlessly disputed private land titles that can be traced back to the conquest, and a relatively impoverished majority of *comuneros*, who collectively own and farm common lands. The private title holders are descended from the Spanish colonists and

Chuquibamba. A classic Spanish pueblo, Chuquibamba nestles idyllically in the valley of the Chacahuayco.

the Chachapoya elite who intermarried with them; the *comuneros* embody the persistence of pre-Columbian peasant society. Needless to say, political tensions are evident, but personal and economic relationships are generally harmonious, although an overabundance of cheap *aguardiente* from Pusak does ignite occasional discord.

Pelayo Jáuregui is a member of one of Chuquibamba's wealthier families. With his help, I have been able to develop a network of information and support that has expanded over the years to include both private landowners and *comuneros*. In this endeavor, I had both a predecessor and an excellent model: before I arrived, Chuquibamba was the home away from home of Inge Schjellerup, a philanthropist as well as an archaeologist and ethnographer. Her willingness to share her profound knowledge of her research territory, as well as her understanding of the people who live within it, has been exceptionally generous.

Neighboring Uchucmarca, about a day's ride away, is almost identical to Chuquibamba except that it was recently connected to the outside world by a vehicular road—or, rather, the unpaved, bone-jarring parody of one. In many respects, the two towns operate symbiotically, in a modern expression of the traditional bipolar organization of Andean societies, bound by culture and by blood ties, and rivals in everything from soccer to landownership.

Chuquibamaba. Traces of glaze identify this mustachioed ceramic effigy from the Chacahuayco drainage as a postconquest work. The bizarre gesture and facial expression suggest pain and disease. Perhaps this effigy portrays a victim of the disease uta, *which plagued native as well as European populations when they established villages at lower elevations than the Chachapoya had more wisely occupied.*

Uchucmarca is the family home of Peruvian archaeologist Abel Vega Ocampo, who has also helped me generously in recent years.

Much has changed in both these towns since pre-Columbian times, but much has remained the same. Although Catholicism has replaced indigenous beliefs, vestiges of ancient customs still assert themselves, as when drinkers propitiate the Earth with the final drops of every cup of *aguardiente*. Mules, able to carry double the weight of llamas, have replaced them as beasts of burden, but most loads are borne on the backs of the people. Cattle, sheep, goats, pigs, and chickens have been introduced along with wheat and barley, yet potatoes, corn, and beans are still the staples of the *comuneros'* diet, and *cuy* scavenge kitchen floors for scraps that fall from the tables that they themselves will eventually grace. Spanish tile is used to roof municipal buildings and the homes of wealthier citizens; *ichu*—bunchgrass thatch—is still employed in the outlying parts of town.

The subsistence patterns of both communities are fundamentally the same as before the Spanish arrived. They depend on simultaneous exploitation of the varied climates and products of the vertically stacked environments above, below, and around them. Each community, having control over a complete spectrum of essential produce, is largely independent of the outside world and (to borrow a term from the anthropological literature) constitutes an economic archipelago. It is this subsistence pattern that enabled the ancient Chachapoya communities to be so politically autonomous but also allowed the Inka to pick them off one by one.

To live in these towns is to be transported back to the Middle Ages. As I wander around Chuquibamba and Uchucmarca, I often ponder how little life would change if the outside world simply vanished. The light of a few kerosene lanterns would be dimmed, a transistor radio or two would be silenced, and feet would no longer be shod with tire-soled sandals, but the basic quality and tempo of life would scarcely be altered.

It would be easy—indeed, it is tempting—to romanticize the existence of these rural people. In certain respects, I deeply envy their communal existence, the simplicity of their lives, their daily physical exercise, their quarantine from technology, their immunity to information overload, and, above all, the depth of their emotions. Yet the truth is also that they will grieve the death of one in every three of their children before the children reach the age of five, that the survivors will suffer from intestinal parasites for most of their lives, that some will die from curable diseases for lack of rudimentary medical attention, that hard labor will condemn others to an arthritic old age, and that they will always know of a more affluent world outside, which abandons them to their poverty. In their own poignant phrase, they live in *pueblos olvidados*, forgotten towns. Like most other Peruvians, they exist in a dispiriting purgatory, desperately supplicating benefits of the industrial world, which are promised but never arrive, while experiencing deep nostalgia for an ancient and more dignified culture that was irretrievably lost before they could experience it. In the course of their labor, they continuously encounter ancient buildings, tombs, and artifacts. After overcoming their initial suspicions and fears of the evil spirits said to inhabit ancient ruins,

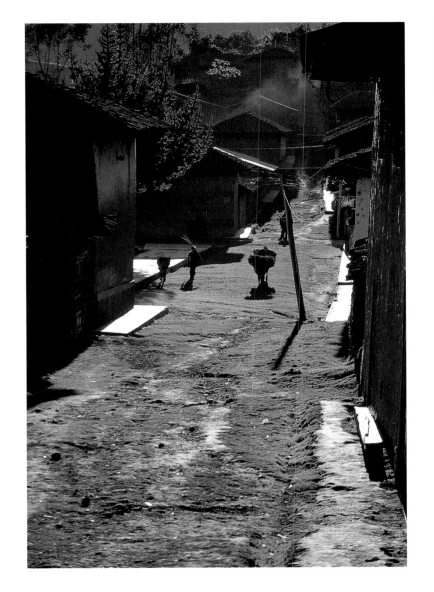

Chuquibamba. Everyday life in Chuquibamba has barely changed in three hundred years. With no vehicles, there is no need to pave the roads, which turn to pasture during the rainy season.

Chuquibamba. Chuquibamba has no resident priest. A small community of nuns of the Convento Patmos attends to the spiritual needs of the population and dispenses donations of clothing and medicine.

Chuquibamba. Time stands still in Chuquibamba. The date of the foundation of its church has been forgotten, but its twin in nearby Uchucmarca bears an inscription that dates it to 1692. I was in Chuquibamba when the church was being repaired. I asked how long it took to reroof it. After some discussion, my informants agreed on forty years. They were including the time it had taken to grow eucalyptus trees to replace the termite-ridden timbers.

Chuquibamba. My expeditions from Chuquibamba always depart with saddlebags stuffed with fresh-baked bread from Leilde Vergaray's clay ovens.

they proudly show me the sites they have found, and they lament the destruction wrought by half their ancestors on the other half.

THE CHACAHUAYCO AND PUSAK SITES

Chuquibamba is surrounded by the ruins of several ancient Chachapoya settlements. A sheltered slope halfway up the flank of the mountain that overlooks Chuquibamba is the site of Gentil; a ridge is occupied by the ruins of Patrón Samana; and there are buildings at Runa Shayana, near the summit. In the highlands between Chuquibamba and Uchucmarca are several ruined villages. Pueblo Viejo, or Chibul, which enjoys a spectacular panorama of the Marañón valley, is not one but two adjacent semifortified ruins, apparently the "upper" and "lower" social divisions of a single community. The lower of the two is known as Churo. This juxtaposition of two sites, or the division of a site into two distinct components, occurs at several Chachapoya ruins, notably at Kuelap, and is an architectural expression of the pan-Andean principle of dual social organization. Pueblo Viejo has a high proportion of large-diameter buildings, some with interior niches, benches, and subdividing walls. Pomio, which occupies two prominences and the saddle between them, overlooks Uchucmarca. Although no longer "littered with fallen sculptures," as Gene Savoy described it, Pomio is in open grasslands, so its few fallen *cabezas clavas* are relatively easy to find.

Above Uchucmarca there is a plethora of archaeological sites. Most impressive is Pirca Pirca, which is distinguished by a unique rectangular building of singularly ambitious proportions for the Chachapoya sphere of influence. One hundred and seventy feet long, forty feet wide, and over forty feet high, this building incorporates beehive-shaped, corbeled vaults, presumably tombs, long since looted.

Chuquibamba. A youthful muleteer wears a style of poncho that identifies him as a Chuquibambino.

Chuquibamba. In a Chuquibamba schoolroom, kids wave toothbrushes donated by my dentist. I didn't realize that one child failed to get hers until I looked closely at this photo. Her expression is a poignant reminder that charity can inadvertently cause pain.

Chuquibamba. For threshing wheat in the fields above Chuquibamba, an improvised corral is enclosed with rope hung with ponchos, and mules are driven around and around to trample the harvest and separate the grain from the chaff.

Chuquibamba. Dressed in their Sunday best, two Chuquibambinas were intercepted on their way to decorate the church for the annual fiesta patronal.

Cajamarca. The face of a campesino embodies five hundred years of profoundly melancholy consequences of European interactions with native American populations.

Expanded over time in clearly distinguishable phases, this building was constructed on the barely discernible foundations of an earlier circular structure. Its upper surface is paved with flagstones that must weigh several tons—some of them are over nine feet long by three feet wide and eighteen inches thick. The building is mostly constructed of white limestone; its cornices and upper pavement are highlighted with alternating red sandstone and black slate ashlars. These, although they have now weathered to a neutral gray, must originally have given the building a rhythmically geometric appearance. Curiously, the building was once capped by a round building at one end and a square one at the other, thus breaching the Chachapoya canon of bilateral symmetry while epitomizing the persistent Chachapoya theme of opposition and complementarity. Conceivably, the juxtaposition of a circular structure with a rectangular one might even be a concrete expression of a political accommodation between the Chachapoya and the Inka. Near this impressive monument is a large community of round houses, made of randomly shaped but carefully assembled field stones set in clay mortar (the type of masonry called *pirca*). Many of these houses have underground storage cysts. Uchucmarquinos assert that they are all connected to an underground tunnel linking Kuelap and Cuzco!

Farther up the Pusak, opposite the modern village of Las Quinuas and not far south of the convergence of the ridges that separate the Pusak, Chacahuayco, and Utcubamba watersheds, is an especially attractive cluster of ruins known as Las Ruinas Frente a Urbano, or Los Caserones. This site is constructed almost entirely of the high-quality red sandstone reserved in most other places for geometric decorations and *cabezas clavas*. Framed against the backdrop of a white limestone cliff, it must once have presented a rich contrast of colors. Although the buildings are mostly round and Chachapoya in spirit, the tightly fitted masonry and the use of stone that had to be brought in from a considerable distance both suggest an Inka influence. According to Espinoza Soriano, an Inka "puppet" Chachapoya ruler, Apo Chuquimis (who was once a favorite of Huayna Cápac but was later accused of poisoning him) occupied a palatial estate in Las Quinuas. Perhaps this was Apo Chuquimis's residence.

ATUÉN AND THE PASSES TO THE EASTERN *MONTAÑA*

The source of the Utcubamba is a winding lake, La Sierpe, which is apparently fed by underground streams from a higher lake called Mishacocha. Highland lakes, or *cochas*, were and still are believed to be enchanted and imbued with metaphysical powers, especially if they are the sources of important rivers. The Chachapoya apparently valued access to and views of *cochas*, and ancient communities are often found close to them. La Sierpe is no exception. On the ridges and slopes around La Sierpe are numerous Chachapoya sites, such as the walled ruins of Cabildo Pata and the ruins of Peña Calata. At the margin of the lake is an Inka ruin, now largely incorporated into the contemporary village of Atuén.

Atuén, an abbreviation of Jatun Llacta Sierpe (Important Village at Serpent Lake), is built entirely from reassembled Inka stone blocks. One or two of its houses, as Victor W. von Hagen noted, seem to be original Inka structures still in use.

Ancient Atuén, strategically located just below and to the north of the important pass that separates the Pusak drainage from the Utcubamba, was an Inka military garrison. Colorful local myths recount, in graphic detail, pitched battles between the Chachapoya of Cabildo Pata and Peña Calata and the Inka invaders, who swooped down from the pass, costumed as pumas and condors, yelling "Ululul-lilili-lalala!"—thus giving the pass, the Fila de Ulila, its name. Since the Fila de Ulila physically divides the northern and southern halves of Chachapoya territory, the Chachapoya surely would have made a stand there against the Inka. Perhaps the folklore of Atuén recalls the battle for Papamarca, which Garcilaso de la Vega tells us took place somewhere between Cajamarquilla and Leimebamba. In any event, evidence for Inka conquest and occupancy of the area is unambiguous. Where La Sierpe drains into the Utcubamaba there is an Inka bath, now sadly neglected but virtually intact, with characteristic trapezoidal niches—almost as if the Inka bathers needed somewhere to set down their soap and washcloths. Local tradition claims that Huayna Cápac bathed here every day while recuperating from an illness.

Chuquibamba. The ruins of Gentil.

Uchucmarca. A rectangular building above Uchucmarca at Pirca Pirca is probably the largest freestanding structure in the Chachapoya region.

Uchucmarca. This site, in the headwaters of the Pusak above Uchucmarca near Las Quinuas, is finely constructed from imported red sandstone. Its buildings elegantly blend rectangular and curvilinear forms. Gregorio Añazco, an authority from Atuén on folklore and herbal medicine, has discovered that a hard hat is ideal headgear for the local climate—and can double as a drinking bowl.

Uchucmarca. This monument from Pirca Pirca, along with many other from nearby sites, is now in Uchucmarca. Regrettably, most portable artifacts such as this one have long since been removed by collectors.

Atuén today is a rather bleak and solitary place with a handful of inhabitants, some of whom, although cash-poor, run large herds of cattle in open rangelands above the village. I have the honor of being *padrino*, or godfather, to two of Atuén's children—a relationship that was solemnized when I became the first person to cut a lock of their hair.

Atuén. Atuén, at the source of the Utcubamba, is made of recycled Inka building material. The buildings and terraces of the fortress of Torre Pukro outline the summit in the center of the photograph.

CHAPTER FIVE

Exploring the Eastern Montaña

In addition to guarding the Fila de Ulila, Atuén was undoubtedly of strategic importance in controlling access to and from the eastern *montaña,* which was then inhabited by a subgroup of the Chachapoya called the Chilcho. The Chilcho must have acted as both a buffer and a conduit between the highland Chachapoya and the lowland tribes. As inhabitants of a transitional zone, they probably blended highland with lowland cultural traits.

From a historical and archaeological point of view, the Chilcho are virtually unknown. For several years, I had been collecting (and wanting to confirm) reports of ruins and cliff tombs in the *montaña.* Penetrating the *montaña* was to prove complicated, however, as well as arduous, because a craggy and notoriously inhospitable cordillera separates Atuén from the *montaña.* An unwary traveler can all too easily become lost there in thick mists, stumble from bog to bog, and die of exposure. In fact, my curiosity almost consigned me to that fate.

THE *MONTAÑA: REGIÓN INEXPLORADA*

On the maps of the nineteenth-century naturalist and cartographer Antonio Raimondi, who was by far the greatest explorer Peru has ever known, almost the entire area between the Central Cordillera and the Huallaga is marked *Región inexplorada*—about five thousand square miles of unexplored territory. More recent Peruvian government maps confidently fill this territory in with blue dendrites representing the courses of rivers, but these maps are grossly unreliable. Better maps are rumored to exist, but if they do, they are withheld from the public: Peruvian authorities do not want them to fall into the hands of the guerrillas and drug traffickers who infest the upper reaches of the Huallaga valley, where illicit coca plantations supply the raw material for the world's cocaine trade and finance violent revolutionary movements. Satellite photos are readily available but are difficult to interpret because of the dense vegetation and cloud cover. In short, the topography of the *montaña* is scarcely better known now than it was a century ago.

Gran Pajatén. In this mosaic frieze at Gran Pajatén, the addition of the headdress and other features around the cabeza clava shows a pattern unique to the southern montaña. Photograph by Juan-Tomás Rehbock.

77

The northern sector of Raimondi's *Región inexplorada* lies generally to the south and east of the modern town of Rodriguez de Mendoza. It is drained by the Huambo and its tributaries. The cordillera there is easily crossed, so the fringes of the *montaña* have been continuously inhabited from pre-Columbian times. Pre-Columbian ruins on the upper Huambo were reported by Vidal Senèze in the late nineteenth century, and in the 1940s they were systematically recorded by a Peruvian archaeological official, Victor Zubiate. Gene Savoy, working from Zubiate's reports, mounted expeditions into the area and claimed sensational discoveries during the 1960s. It was in this area that I first explored Chachapoya remains, in the early 1970s. More recently, Morgan Davis, Peter Lerche, and others have greatly expanded the list of documented sites on the upper Huambo, but the lower reaches are still archaeologically unsurveyed.

The southern sector of Raimondi's *Región inexplorada*, which is more difficult of access, is drained by a poorly mapped system of rivers that have been given a dizzying array of names. The major rivers are usually (but not invariably) called the Jepelache, the Pajatén, and the Abiseo. All these eventually join together before flowing into the Huallaga. Much of this region, too, remains unexplored, but investigation of the Abiseo and its tributaries has already produced some uniquely interesting ruins of Chachapoya buildings. Traces of ancient roads heading east from known ruins on the western side of the cordillera—including sites near Piás, Condormarca, and Cajamarquilla (today Bolívar), the first three Chachapoya population centers overrun by the Inka—provide clear evidence of Chachapoya contact with the *montaña*. Incidental reports by botanists, prospectors, and surveyors, dating

at least as far back as the 1920s, when Weberbauer followed Inka roads passing several ancient sites, had confirmed that the region contained pre-Columbian remains. Nevertheless, archaeologists seem to have assumed that the *montaña* thereabouts was a virtually impassable and uninhabitable barrier between the highland and lowland cultures.

This assumption was resoundingly contradicted by the discovery in 1964, by a trio of Peruvian explorers led by the mayor of Pataz, Carlos Torrealva Juárez, of a spectacular group of ruins now known as Gran Pajatén (after the abandoned Spanish colonial mission of Pajatén, which once existed in the vicinity). Gene Savoy soon heard of the find, visited the site, and brought back captivating photographs of a cluster of Chachapoya buildings with ornate stone-mosaic friezes and an unusual abundance of *cabezas clavas*.

Subsequent explorations have revealed additional sites, including a group of pristine Chachapoya tombs at Los Pinchudos (vernacular for The Pricks), which Savoy photographed from the air but apparently never reached on foot. One of the tombs at Los Pinchudos is decorated with well-preserved (and well-endowed) wooden figures that have been studied by the foremost Peruvian authority on cliff tombs, Federico Kauffmann Doig. What is most baffling about Gran Pajatén and Los Pinchudos is that they exhibit the most highly developed expression of the Chachapoya architectural repertoire, which one might reasonably expect to find in the heartland of Chachapoya territory but not on its periphery.

Meanwhile, however, the central sector of Raimondi's *Región inexplorada*, drained by the Huabayacu and its tributaries, remained archaeologically unknown. Like the rest of the *montaña*, it is difficult terrain: mountainous, thickly forested, subject to heavy rainfall, and incised by torrential rivers that have cut steep canyons in its predominantly sedimentary rock; a landscape Peruvians call *muy accidentado*. Scant archival references to it indicate that it was once occupied by the Chilcho. There are vague allusions to its having been used as a place of refuge for Chachapoya fleeing the Inka and, later, the Spanish. Local legends assert that the Inka Huayna Cápac once made his way through it from Atuén to Moyobamba, the extreme northeastern limit of Chachapoya influence. Not long after the Spanish conquest, the combination of the catastrophic collapse of the Chachapoya and the ravages of Old World diseases decimated the population. Franciscan missionaries in the seventeenth and eighteenth centuries, at lower elevations close to the Huallaga, encountered only the Hivito, a tribe probably unrelated to the Chilcho. They converted some of these people and cajoled them into mission settlements; others remained hostile and forced the Franciscans to abandon this territory. By the nineteenth century, the Huabayacu drainage was virtually if not totally uninhabited. Any vestiges of the Chilcho subgroup of the Chachapoya remained unseen and untouched for over a century.

MODERN PIONEERS OF THE *MONTAÑA*

Gran Pajatén was discovered by farmers who were exploring the eastern *montaña* in search of new agricultural land. Having undertaken their explorations deliberately, they realized the significance of their archaeological discovery and promptly reported it to the Peruvian authorities. They had actively sought out ancient remains, especially agricultural terraces, because they knew from experience that these were infallible indicators of cultivable land. As their initial report made clear, they were well aware of earlier settlements in the *montaña*, settlements they might have read about in *The Serpent of Gold*, Ciro Alegría's classic 1935 novel of life on the Marañón:

> Years ago, many years ago, there was a road, but later the jungle swallowed it up completely. Those were the days when they used to do business with Pajatén, Pachiza, Uchiza and all those towns, and with the Cholones and Hivitos too. But the Indians started massacring the Christians. The pueblo of Pajatén disappeared, maybe because the Indians destroyed it, or maybe just because of the fear of them.

At approximately the same time that the discoverers of Gran Pajatén were probing the southern sector of Raimondi's *Región inexplorada*, similar groups of pioneers were exploring its northern and central sectors. In the north, trails descending the Huambo were being opened, and in the central sector, the cordillera was being crossed at several places as efforts were made to extract timber from and to introduce cattle into the Huabayacu drainage.

The most persistent and significant penetration into the Huabayacu drainage was spearheaded by Benigno Añazco, a reclusive, near-legendary explorer who embarked, as a teenager in the 1940s, on a heroic quest to discover a route to connect Atuén with the Huallaga and, from there, to the navigable rivers of the

Amazon basin. In this romantic ambition, and in his lifetime of trailblazing accomplishments, Benigno Añazco bears an astonishingly close resemblance to the fictional protagonist of Gabriel García Márquez's masterpiece *One Hundred Years of Solitude*, of whom we are told: "In his youth, José Arcadio Buendía and his men, with wives and children, animals, and all kinds of domestic implements, crossed the mountains in search of an outlet to the sea."

Benigno Añazco departed from Atuén and crossed the cordillera in pursuit of his vision. In the course of the next fifty years, he painstakingly established a chain of homesteads (populated by his rapidly multiplying descendants) along the upper reaches of the Huabayacu. Along the way, he uncovered a succession of Chachapoya, Inka, and Spanish colonial remains, to which he assigned such romantic names as Osiris, Brillante Luna, Casa de Oro, Orfedón, Israel, and Vilcabamba. Eventually, he found a level pampa large enough to accommodate an embryonic settlement that he called La Morada. But, being restless, he bequeathed this to his wife and children and moved on. In recent years, he has reached another pampa and has established a new community at La Meseta. Here, too, on an ancient road that evidently linked the Chachapoya communities along the eastern side of the cordillera, he uncovered a small but exceptionally well constructed imperial Inka shrine. In essence, Benigno Añazco, his family, and their cattle, which he himself credits with forging new trails, opened up thousands of square miles of *montaña* to settlement and provided access to an important new zone of archaeological discoveries.

THE HUABAYACU SITES

Unfortunately, Benigno Añazco and his clan were not well disposed toward gringos like me. Gene Savoy's campaigns, which included mountaineering expeditions into the tombs at La Petaca and underwater reconnaissance of several highland lakes, had led to the widespread belief that he, along with every other foreigner, was a looter. I do not believe that myself. I had interviewed Savoy and several of his guides and companions, and I had come to the conclusion that Savoy was a reasonably scrupulous investigator. My opinions were not the operative ones, however.

In addition to the warranted xenophobia of a people whose history is one of outside exploitation, the Añazcos had, as I gradually learned, other reasons to preserve their isolation from the rest of the world. They were adherents of the Seventh-Day Adventist faith, members of a minority religion who were endeavoring to create a safe haven for their beliefs. Moreover, Benigno Añazco was wanted by the authorities on charges of incest and murder. Having fathered a family with his wife, he took his own daughter as his mate, like a character from the Old Testament, and became the progenitor of a second family. Furthermore, he had shot and killed one of the settlers who followed in his footsteps, either for molesting one of his daughters or, according to another variant of the story, for planting coca and opium poppies and thereby putting the population at risk from the drug traffickers.

My initial efforts, in 1987, to enter the Huabayacu drainage and

The Huabayacu. After we crested the Andes and descended through frigid jalca, a sweeping panorama of the upper Huabayacu came into view. Benigno Añazco's first homestead, Sitio Alegre, appears as a speck on the landscape at the foot of the valley. Beyond it lies the forested ceja de la montaña.

photograph the sites rumored to exist between Atuén and La Morada were received with hostility and repeatedly frustrated. Before leaving Chuquibamba, I was interrogated by a tribunal that questioned my credentials, cast doubt on my motives, and denied me permission to proceed. Having crossed—or, rather, sidestepped—that hurdle by obtaining dispensation from the higher authorities in Chachapoyas, I went to Atuén, where my diplomatic overtures to the Añazco colonists were coldly rejected by Benigno's oldest son, Zacarías, whose eyes never once met mine. The envelope containing my authorization was handed back to me unopened, supposedly because it was improperly sealed, and I was assumed to have tampered with the contents. I was never physically threatened, but Pelayo and my local informant, Gregorio Añazco, were unambiguously notified that my presence was unwelcome. Armed guards, they were warned, had been posted to ensure that I would not get over the cordillera. Next morning, I awoke to find that our mules had inexplicably escaped from their corral during the night. All but one of the indolent beasts had remained in the area, but it still took several hours to round them up. My favorite saddle mule, Lucera, however, had left a trail of hoofprints notifying us that she was well on her way back to her pasture in Chuquibamba. This was not an auspicious beginning.

Fortunately, a *fiesta* was about to take place in Leimebamba. *Fiestas* are normally the bane of the traveler's existence, since all commerce and traffic come to a complete halt for days. But in this instance the fiesta was a boon: I was absolutely certain that no self-respecting Peruvian would squander an opportunity to carouse

Jardín. Smoke billows from our campfire in the "Jardín Hilton," a tambo on the trail to La Morada.

Jardín. In the ceja around Jardín, every tree becomes the armature of an ecosystem, supporting hundreds of other plant species and myriad insects.

with friends and family in Leimebamba by waiting on the trail to intercept me. Seizing this brief opportunity to get over the cordillera and back with no interference, I decided to undertake a swift reconnaissance. In the bitter cold of a predawn morning, the remaining mules were loaded and we slipped quietly out of Atuén.

We passed La Sierpe and the Laguna Mishacocha, pausing to catch our breath at Peña del Retrato, where there are a few small pictographs. The trail up and over the inappropriately named Pasa Breve (Short Pass) was bleak and broken, with treacherous potholes and crevices in the limestone that were liable to break our animals' legs if they misstepped (contrary to popular belief, mules are not invariably surefooted). We crossed the cordillera before noon, alternately pummeled by cyclonic gusts of wind and pelted with hailstones. Garcilaso de la Vega's description of the death by freezing of three hundred elite Inka troops, under similar conditions during the war against the Chachapoya, became all too believable.

But our rewards were proportional to our pains. As we descended the eastern flank of the Central Cordillera, a magnificent sun-dappled vista of the forested Huabayacu valley, animated by the shadows of fast-moving clouds spiraling up the valley, spread out below us. Far away, we could see Benigno Añazco's first homestead, Sitio Alegre, little more than a speck on the landscape. By nightfall, we had passed it and had reached an idyllic place in the *ceja de la montaña* aptly named Jardín, the Garden of Eden. We camped in a primitive lean-to shelter, the Añazcos' roadside *tambo*, which we baptized the Jardín Hilton.

Despite its lack of creature comforts, Jardín was a veritable paradise of orchids, bromeliads, fuchsias, daturas, and stately tree ferns. Every plant was an ecosystem teeming with smaller plants and insects. Orchids ranged from clusters of microscopic blossoms less than an eighth of an inch in diameter to flowering spikes over six feet long. I estimated that no fewer than fifty varieties of orchid would be found within a hundred-yard radius of the *tambo*. As I dozed fitfully during the moonlit night, wondering if the Añazcos would discover us, an oilbird, a nocturnal echolocator that nests in caves in the *montaña*, buzzed my sleeping loft, making incongruous quacking noises.

By noon the following day, after fording the river half a dozen times, we reached our first objective: the Cueva de Osiris. The name Osiris is apparently a pun, referring both to the Egyptian deity of Benigno's prophetic fantasies and to *osos de anteojos*, the bespectacled-looking bears he had to evict from it. Across the canyon, high above the fast-moving river, a wooden balcony projected from a ledge that also housed the remnants of a circular masonry tomb. Above the balcony was a profusion of red pictographs, considerably more than I had ever seen on the western side of the cordillera. Most were targetlike designs—open circles with solid bull's-eyes in the center. There were also two anthropomorphic figures, one of which was very sharply delineated and had a targetlike head. I worked frantically with the telephoto equipment, trying to rid the lenses of condensation before the sun, which intermittently illuminated the rock art, permanently disappeared behind the menacing clouds. Meanwhile, Pelayo and Gregorio hacked away at the vegetation to give me a clearer line of sight.

jalca into the forested *ceja*. By the time we finally reached the shelter of the Jardín Hilton, torrential rains had turned it into an atoll in a sea of mud.

The following day dawned clear but humid. Anticipating a long day's journey, we broke camp quickly. We passed Cueva de Osiris without setting up the tripod because the air in the canyon was too full of vapor for telephotography. A short distance below Osiris, however, the river Yonán joins the Huabayacu, and near their union I excitedly photographed La Brillante Luna (Shining Moon), the most impressive complex of cliff tombs I had witnessed since La Petaca.

Brillante Luna has masonry tombs with zigzag friezes, plastered and painted with alternating bands of red and white and accompanied by the now familiar targetlike designs and stick-figure anthropomorphs. The similarities to La Petaca were obvious, but so were the differences, especially the prevalence of the pictographs. Protruding from one of the tombs were bundles of wooden staves with carved ends—possibly the cross members of a collapsed roof, notched for lashings, but also suggestive of spears or bows, as if the building had served as an arsenal. Even with two tele-extenders on my most powerful lenses, I was barely able to capture the details, and the heat haze hindered the photography.

Downriver, the course of the Huabayacu is paralleled by an Inka road that comes down the valley of the Yonán from a pass that leads to Cajamarquilla. The old pre-Columbian bridge spanning the Huabayacu had disappeared, but the Añazcos had replaced it with an Inka-inspired suspension bridge, ingeniously made of twisted wire. High on a cliff above the Yonán, we could distinguish a spectacular tomb, barely visible in the distance, emblazoned with a single crisply executed targetlike emblem. Benigno Añazco had dubbed this Casa de Oro (House of Gold). It was too far away to photograph without a detour over the Añazcos' treacherous-looking bridge, so we crossed it one at a time, with great trepidation. Scanning the cliffs opposite Casa de Oro, we spotted another tomb, with typical interlocking Chachapoya geometric designs beneath its doorway. This perfectly preserved structure could barely be discerned with binoculars and had apparently escaped even the Añazcos' keen eyesight. Farther downriver, beyond the abutments of the old Inka bridge, I was shown two additional clusters of tombs, one called Boca Mina (it is near an ancient mine) and the other called Tres Ojos (one of the buildings is decorated with three concentric designs).

We recrossed the flimsy wire bridge and followed the Inka road down the Huabayacu, passing through a zone of ancient agricultural terraces with retaining walls up to ten feet high, until we reached Orfedón, another of Benigno's former homesteads. Orfedón sits on a bluff above the river, alongside the remains of several ancient circular foundations. To the north of Orfedón are promising cliffs, where I learned that more tombs had been found, and where *chonta* palm spears had been collected in the debris of

Tres Ojos. Eyner Añazco, with his brother Salustiano, guided me to this complex of tombs on the upper Huabayacu. Along with Zacarías Añazco, they first saw it in 1988 and dubbed it Tres Ojos (Three Eyes). To the right and slightly below it is another painted tomb, which still has most of its second story and doorway intact. Nearby, the Huabayacu narrows to a deep gorge, where the abutments of the pre-Columbian bridge that once spanned it can still be seen. A spur road leads to an ancient mine and to another cluster of tombs at Boca Mina.

Pampa Hermosa. Pre-Columbian people excelled in the construction of suspension bridges made from twisted plant fibers. Taking a leaf out of their ancestors' book but adopting modern materials, the Añazcos spanned the Huabayacu at Pampa Hermosa with baling wire. This bridge was subsequently swept away in the aftermath of an earthquake and landslide and was reduced to a few pathetically twisted strands trapped between the gigantic boulders that had roared down the valley, destroying everything in their path. Miraculously, no lives were lost.

Puerto. Minutes after I took this picture, the decaying balcony at Puerto collapsed under the weight of my saddle mule, Lucera. In building this cantilevered road, Benigno Añazco was inspired by Chachapoya engineers. Unfortunately, he did not possess their knowledge of rot-resistant woods.

The trail to La Morada. Fabian Añazco, second son of Benigno and mayor of La Morada, clears the trail while a cargo mule waits apprehensively. Trails in the montaña are twisting tunnels through the vegetation, so diminutive mules, like the pit ponies of Welsh coal mines, are bred to thread their way through them.

fallen structures. Given the scale of the terracing that we had passed through, it was indisputable that the area had once supported a large population. Our river-valley trail was ideal for observing the profusion of orchids and bromeliads, as well as the cacophonous flocks of birds that feasted in the treetops, but I believed that we were bypassing the most significant ruins, which I felt certain would be found on the unexplored ridges above us.

Continuing on toward La Morada, we were intermittently doused by the sudden cloudbursts characteristic of the *ceja*. At a place called Puerto, the trail skirted the river, which was about twenty or thirty feet below. Here, a section of the Inka road reopened by Benigno Añazco had been washed away by the river, so, borrowing from the repertoire of the Chachapoya engineers, he had wedged horizontal beams into the cliff to create a cantilevered causeway. Respecting the fragility of this arrangement, we unloaded the mules and lugged both cargo and harnesses across the bridge, in order to reduce the weight on the decaying wooden platform. I was sent ahead with the cargo, to barricade the trail and prevent the mules from escaping. I signaled that I was in position, and then I heard a commotion.

Below me, Pelayo and Fabian, clinging to one of the mules, were being swept downriver. The mule struggled desperately against the strong current but ran aground on some rocks. As Pelayo and Fabian wrestled the frantic mule toward relatively firm ground, I realized that it was Lucera: she had broken through the planking and tumbled into the river. High water had cushioned the blow and spared her life, but the hide along her back was split open near her tail, exposing several vertebrae. She was bleeding profusely, and I could see fragments of bone that had been shattered by the impact.

Pelayo and Fabian wanted to put Lucera out of her misery immediately. I persuaded them to see if she could walk: she could. Through increasingly torrential downpours, we proceeded toward Benigno's next settlement, Israel, hoping to find salvation there. Lucera, ears pinned back, trudged stoically along, kicking and snapping at anyone or any mule imprudent enough to get too close. Because Lucera's saddle had to be loaded on top of Fabian's mule's saddle, we lost the use of both animals. Pelayo and I slogged on miserably through the morass that passed for a trail. While Fabian, accustomed to the trail, strode confidently from root to root, I learned to fall face down in the mud rather than grab the nearest plant, which was likely to be armored with vicious spines. True to the long tradition of Amazonian exploration, I literally plunged headlong into the jungle. Whenever the rain abated, the sun beat down, and Lucera's wound would quickly become covered with flies. I packed her wound with an improvised poultice of iodine, antibiotics, mosquito repellent, and everything else I thought might help, but the next downpour would flush the mixture out. Sheets of running water were undermining the trees that blocked the trail every few hundred yards, and Fabian expertly cleared the way, using a long-handled ax on any timber that resisted his machete.

Israel. Pelayo inspects an Inka bath at Israel.

Israel. An enormous sandstone monolith, approximately twelve feet by five feet by three feet, is engraved with enigmatic designs of unknown cultural origin. The bedrock source of this material is several miles away, so it seems unlikely that a boulder this size could have arrived here without human intervention. Whether the designs were carved before or after the monolith reached Israel is an open question. The Inka and other pre-Columbian people worshipped such rocks and referred to them, along with other sacred objects, as huacas. This, presumably, is one of the huacas of Israel.

The disaster of Lucera's injury was mitigated by the archaeological excitement of Israel—which, surprisingly for its location, is an Inka site. Inge Schjellerup had already cleared and surveyed the central part of the ruin, revealing two Inka house compounds, or *kanchas*, a larger building of the type known as a *kallanka*, two well-preserved Inka baths, and a defensive wall. Together, these testified that this had been an Inka *tambo* and administrative center of some importance. The presence of an Inka site this far beyond the previously confirmed extent of Inka influence in the *montaña* was not just surprising; it lent credence to the rumors of Inka polygonal masonry farther down the Huabayacu, at La Meseta.

Among the remains at Israel was an engraved stone about the size and shape of a doorjamb or lintel. The figures on it were not of recognizably Inka origin. They bore greater resemblance to the anthropomorphic paintings on the cliffs, and to the interlocking geometric motifs of the Chachapoya friezes. One carving juxtaposed curvilinear and rectilinear interlocking designs—another manifestation of the oppositional themes that permeate ancient Andean imagery. Nearby, also engraved with cryptic designs, lay a red sandstone monolith weighing several tons. The material from which this monument was carved was not of local origin. Therefore, unless it had come to rest at its present location after some primordial landslide, it must have been transported a considerable distance overland, or by river—a testimonial to the pan-Andean reverence for stone. The Añazcos had named the Inka ruins at Israel Puka Rumi (in Quechua, Red Rock) in honor of this landmark. Since most of the motifs on both of these engraved monuments were not familiar to me as Inka designs, I guessed that they might be examples of the well-documented Inka practice of co-opting the *huacas*, or sacred monuments, of conquered people and holding them hostage.

After photographing the site and recuperating overnight at Israel, we resumed our journey until we reached an even more remarkable site, at Hornopampa. Hornopampa's main feature is a large, solidly constructed, well-preserved circular building almost forty feet in diameter, larger than the vast majority of Chachapoya structures in the highlands and therefore quite unexpected in this region. Its walls are still standing to a height of twelve feet. Unlike any other Chachapoya structure I have ever encountered, it boasts a total of eight large niches: two matching niches on both the interior and exterior walls, on both sides of its entrance. The niches—which

Israel. This stone at Israel juxtaposes rectilinear and curvilinear geometric carvings, a graphic expression of the Andean preoccupation with duality and opposition. Human figures can also be distinguished. The orientation of the designs relative to the shape of the block suggests that it was quarried after the designs were carved. Perhaps this is a huaca *of the Chilcho that was held hostage by the Inka.*

are rectangular, not trapezoidal like Inka niches—probably served as repositories for ritual objects, perhaps sculptures like the wooden figures at Los Pinchudos. Such an imposing building most likely served a ceremonial purpose. I wondered if it might have been a kind of Chachapoya mission, near the frontier of contact with the lowland tribes.

Hornopampa would have been noteworthy for this grandiose Chachapoya building alone, but there was more at which to marvel. Connected to it was a rectangular building about sixty feet long by fifteen feet wide, and not far away was another building of similar proportions, with several doorways along one side. Both of these fit the standard profile of the Inka *kallanka*. Finally, and most surprising of all, the site included the ruin of a diminutive Spanish church with yard-thick walls of mortared stone eight to ten feet high. Running around the interior wall were elevated benches for the congregation and, above them, niches for *santos*. The doorway was particularly interesting to me. It preserved the horizontal shafts that had once held a sliding wooden beam used to bolt the doors. The position of the shaft, on the inside of the recessed jamb, made it clear that the door was intended to be secured from the inside. This had been a place of refuge, then, as well as a place of worship: whoever had prayed here prayed for worldly as well as heavenly salvation.

To date, I have found no record of this mission. It is known that Franciscan missionaries, as early as 1552, had a residence in colonial Chachapoyas, at the site of the old Chachapoya community at Levanto. There is also a brief allusion to a Padre Juan Ramírez from Leimebamba who is said to have converted heathens and built churches in an unspecified part of the *montaña* around

Hornopampa. Fabian Añazco rests after reopening the trail to the ruins of an exceptionally large Chachapoya-style ceremonial building near La Morada

1560. Nevertheless, the first unambiguous reference to missionary activity in this part of the *montaña* is to an unnamed pastor who contacted the Hivito around 1670. Before that, hostile lowland tribes had repeatedly ascended and crossed the cordillera to raid Spanish pueblos on the cordillera's western side. Beginning in 1676, the converted Hivito, along with some of their more numerous southern neighbors, the Cholón, were resettled in a succession of Franciscan missions—Ochanache, Valle, Pajatén, Sión, and Pampa Hermosa. The sites of those missions are farther south, however, and all except Ochanache are known. Furthermore, the siting of a Christian mission at the precise location of an Inka outpost and a Chachapoya ceremonial building would tend to indicate that the church at Hornopampa was established in order to convert people of highland origin, rather than (or in addition to) the lowland Hivito. Therefore, the date of its foundation would probably have been quite soon after the conquest—perhaps a century earlier than the recorded dates of the missions' founding. I am inclined to think that the church at Hornopampa was established by Padre Ramírez. Scientific excavation may tell us one day about this mission's history, from its foundation to its abandonment, as well as about the last remnants of the Inka, the Chilcho faction of the Chachapoya in the *montaña*, and their interactions with the Hivito.

Hornopampa. In this ruin of a Spanish colonial church, the randomly fitted stones, bonded with mortar, differ from the horizontally coursed drywall masonry of the Chachapoya. The wall is now inextricably fused with jungle vegetation.

La Morada. Fabian Añazco and his family dress up and pose for the camera. Though materially poor, they are as full of dignity and as deservedly proud of their accomplishments as any people I know. Here Pelayo and I occupied the penthouse suite, along with an assortment of chickens, turkeys, and bloodsucking parasites.

CHAPTER SIX

The New Chachapoya

Late in the day, we finally arrived at La Morada, a short distance from Hornopampa. The first order of business was to attend to Lucera's infested, infected wound. I cleaned and packed it with antibiotics again and, to the bewilderment of La Morada's inhabitants, sutured it with an upholstery needle and two-pound-test fishing line. If you raise a mule's foreleg, it cannot kick with its hind legs without toppling, so Lucera was easily subdued for the operation. But I wished I had come prepared for bigger fish because the nylon monofilament was barely adequate. With Lucera temporarily patched and out to pasture, Fabian installed us in our quarters.

Our home was the loft of the tallest building in town—the one-and-a-half-story, one-and-a-half-room municipality. This we shared—or, rather, competed for—with half a dozen broody hen turkeys. Pelayo was soon referring to our accommodations as the *rascacielos*, the skyscraper, of La Morada. In the room below, the municipal archives of La Morada were stored in a biscuit tin, sharing a small shelf with a bunch of bananas. The archives revealed that La Morada had been officially founded in 1981 by the family of the illustrious Don Benigno Añazco and had been

carefully laid out with wide streets and an ambitious plan for expansion. Particular care had been invested in the creation of a regulation-size soccer field, which probably occupies the only piece of level ground in at least a fifty-mile radius. To clear this site, tremendous mahogany trees had been felled and burned. In fact, the first death in the village was the consequence of a soccer-field logging accident—a human sacrifice to the sport, which far transcends religion in the number and fanaticism of its devotees in rural Peru.

Some twenty families were already comfortably ensconced in La Morada, with additional settlers clamoring for membership in the community. I wondered aloud why no principal avenue had been named after Benigno and was told that he was refusing the honor until he could be sure that La Morada would not fail. That was the official story, anyway. I sensed that the real reason was the rift caused in the family by Benigno's having taken his daughter as his wife and moved on.

Already, La Morada was bifurcating into two competing factions: the Adventist descendants of Benigno and their relatives from

La Morada. The first essential piece of industrial technology to arrive in La Morada was this antiquated horse-driven trapiche for crushing sugarcane. The next new piece of modern equipment was, unfortunately, a gasoline-powered chain saw. La Morada epitomizes the tension between the compelling economic needs of an impoverished population and the preservation of natural resources.

Atuén and Leimebamba on one side and, on the other, Catholics who were immigrating from Cajamarquilla. The overt bone of contention between them was whether they should play soccer on Saturdays (the Adventists' Sabbath) or on Sundays. At the time of my first visit, there had been only one soccer club. When I returned the following year, in 1989, there were two. In an incident that typifies the unexpected problems encountered by travelers in Peru, this development turned into a political headache for me: I had brought a tournament-quality soccer ball—one ball—as a gift to the community. Both teams coveted the ball, placing me in a Solomon-like predicament. The crisis was resolved diplomatically: I offered it as the prize to whichever team could beat the other in a best-of-

three-games competition. (I doubted that this contest would end amicably, but I knew it would not be finished until after I had left.) Thus the classic dual structure of Andean communities—essential, among other reasons, for the avoidance of inbreeding—was playing itself out through sporting and religious passions, as well as through bloodlines and places of origin. La Morada cries out for a resident anthropologist to chronicle its evolution.

My next destination was to be La Meseta, Benigno Añazco's new settlement two or three days farther down the Huabayacu, where more ruins had been reported, including the Inka polygonal-style shrine. By now my focus was as much on interviewing Benigno himself as on seeing more ruins.

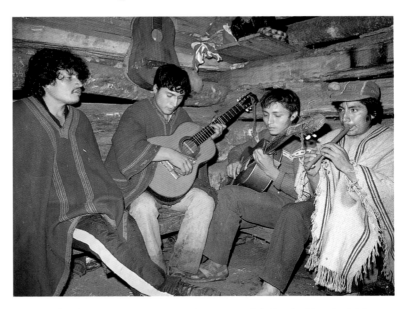

La Morada. An impromptu concert in the municipalidad in La Morada. Moisture-torqued guitar necks must be capoed at the seventh fret, and indestructible Teflon tubing has supplanted perishable materials for the flute. The singers' ballads celebrate Benigno Añazco and plead for the president of Peru, Señor Fujimori, to build a road to La Morada—a somewhat improbable proposition.

La Morada. Zacarías Añazco, eldest son of Benigno, poses with a carved stone Chachapoya artifact unearthed in La Morada. The double-headed snake is a widespread motif in pre-Columbian iconography, as well as in folk mythology. The snake is reputed to lure the unwary hunter to it by imitating a game animal with one of its heads in the treetops, then striking the hunter with the other head, hidden in the grass.

La Morada. Like most other Chachapoya ceramics, this Chachapoya effigy vessel from a tomb near La Morada has zigzag designs around its rim.

101

Fabian Añazco agreed to take me to see his father. We traveled downriver for a day to Cañón Blanco, crossing many *cordones*—low, elongated ridges of fieldstone accumulated during ancient land-clearing operations. At Cañón Blanco, our progress was blocked by high water, which made the route through the gorge impassable—and, unfortunately, time did not permit me to make the necessary detour. Recognizing defeat, I sat down by the bank of the Huabayacu, above the rapids that blocked our way, and dejectedly assembled my telescoping fishing rod. I cast a lure into an eddy that was undercutting the opposite bank and was immediately rewarded by a powerful tug, which bent the rod almost double. For the second time in three days, I wished I had made a less sporting choice of line. But luck was with me, and I landed a specimen trout.

It was some consolation, but Benigno himself continued to elude me. Before returning to La Morada, I wrapped a Spanish-language copy of *One Hundred Years of Solitude* in a plastic bag and left it where Fabian dropped off salt and kerosene for Benigno. I hoped that Benigno would read it and recognize his reflection in the character of José Arcadio Buendía.

Later, Peter Lerche became the first outsider to make contact with Benigno and confirm the existence of the polygonal masonry building. Novelist and journalist Kate Wheeler, guided by Lerche, interviewed Benigno in 1995, so his story has been recorded in his own words for posterity. At this writing, Benigno Añazco remains a fugitive.

CHAPTER SEVEN

Vira Vira

In 1989 and 1990, I mounted two more expeditions into the central sector of Raimondi's *Región inexplorada,* along the Huabayacu and its tributaries above La Morada—making new friends, opening trails, being shown many interesting sites, and hearing of countless others. Pelayo was always with me, and usually Eyner Añazco as well, a bright and energetic young *machetero* from La Morada who became an enthusiastic seeker and protector of the ruins. By some miracle, Lucera had survived her catastrophic fall, and although she now had to wear a special harness to avoid aggravating her injuries, she once again became an excellent saddle mule. Whether my amateur surgery had actually hastened or retarded her recovery I will never know, but she seemed not to hold a grudge, and I was even able to coax her across the treacherous balcony at Puerto. Over the course of these expeditions, as I grasped the extent of the terracing and the number of ancient roads, tombs, mines, and other remains in the valley, I became increasingly convinced that one or more ruined communities awaited discovery somewhere on the ridges separating the Huabayacu's tributaries.

THE LAGUNA HUAYABAMBA

Throughout this phase of my explorations I kept hearing reports of an especially noteworthy highland lake, the Laguna Huayabamba. Like La Sierpe, it was said to be enchanted and was the subject of many legends, most of which involved ghostly apparitions, some benign, others malevolent, emerging from its waters. None of my informants, not even the sagacious Gregorio of Atuén, had actually seen this lake, yet all repeated the same litany: the Laguna Huayabamba was "as round as an orange."

The Laguna Huayabamba evidently was the source of one of many unmapped tributaries of the Huabayacu, to the south of my usual route over the cordillera. My attempts to reach the lake by working my way upriver were frustrated by the difficulties of the terrain, so I decided to traverse the highlands. In 1990 I was guided in this endeavor by Nilo Díaz, the current owner of Benigno Añazco's first homestead at Sitio Alegre, below Pasa Breve. We crossed a windswept ridge well over twelve thousand feet above sea

are reflected and reinforced by the alignment of their architecture. The cosmological orientation of ritually important sites in the Andes is an emerging template that Vira Vira clearly fits.

Doug Sharon's knowledge of the anthropological literature provided other insights that also tended to emphasize the symbolic geometry of the site. Vira Vira's layout divides it into an upper and a lower community, in keeping with patterns already observed at other Chachapoya citadels, notably Kuelap. The terraced gully running down from the large, elaborate buildings in the upper portion of the site conforms with the very ancient Andean tradition of creating U-shaped ceremonial precincts, a practice that dates back as far as the massive preceramic temple mounds of the coast. These U-shaped precincts are often oriented toward sacred mountain peaks or sources of water, and some are believed to have enclosed ritual gardens. Vince and Nancy, while mapping the ceremonial buildings at the head of the gully, found an overgrown spring. Since water from this spring flows to the Laguna Huayabamba and from there to the Huabayacu, it may have been revered by the Chachapoya and used to irrigate ritual gardens below it.

Doug, with his knowledge of traditional medicine, recognized the significance of the name Vira Vira, which is also the name of a plant that is still widely used throughout Peru for preventing and curing bronchial ailments. It now grows wild among the ruins. By a stretch of the imagination, it might even be the plant that was once cultivated in Vira Vira's gardens: *vira* or, in Quechua, *wira* (literally, "fat") is a metaphysical life-force concept that rever-

berates throughout Andean religion, most prominently in the name of the Inka creator deity, Viracocha.

The main pass by which Vira Vira was reached is called Rima Rima, which is also a synonym for a plant with medicinal and ritual significance. According to an oral tradition that I collected during an earlier stay in Atuén, *vira vira* and *rima rima*, both collected from beside the Laguna Huayabamba, were strewn before the conquering Inka Túpac Yupanqui as he led his army over the Fila de Ulila into Atuén. These plants are also credited with curing the Inka Huayna Cápac there when he became ill and bathed in the water from La Sierpe.

Since highland lakes like the Laguna Huayabamba are traditionally places where *curanderos,* or folk healers, gather medicinal herbs, the names Vira Vira and Rima Rima, and their inclusion in legends referring back to the time of the Inka conquest, further underscore the ritual importance of the site. It is possible that Vira Vira is the site's original (or at least its Inka) name. One could even speculate that since the word *cocha* means lake, and since adjacent lakes and communities often have the same root words in their names, the Inka name for the Laguna Huayabamba might have been Viracocha.

In summary, there is reason to think that the inhabitants of Vira Vira conceived of their self-sufficient citadel as a place of healing, a place of creation, and the axis of their natural and cosmological universe.

Vira Vira. Below Vira Vira and around the Laguna Huayabamba, the land was extensively resculpted by the Chachapoya for agriculture. The Vega family, whose homestead, in the foreground, served as base camp for our expeditions, grazes cattle here.

Vira Vira. The edificio principal at Vira Vira is near but not on the summit, a location suggesting that it was a later addition to an already sacred site. Abel Vega and Pelayo Jáuregui inspect the cabeza clava found lying on the surface a few feet away.

On the final evening of our visit, Abel, in a moving toast, described himself as the *portavoz de la naturaleza*, the spokesman of nature, and thanked us for our efforts to bring to light the accomplishments of the noble but long-forgotten Chachapoya, who had conceived and constructed their highland community overlooking the Laguna Huayabamba. Throughout the preceding day, a wildfire set by cattle ranchers on the western side of the cordillera had been cresting it and was now burning relentlessly down the mountainside toward us, voraciously consuming the tinder-dry *ichu*. That night, billowing curtains of smoke glowed an ominous red from the light of the flames beneath them. As we were about to crawl into our tents, we noticed with awe that the fire now formed the outline of a snake, which was poised to strike at our encampment. It was definitely time to leave.

As we parted company with Abel the following morning, storm clouds were looming, and it began to drizzle. "El cielo se pone triste," he said, projecting all our emotions onto the sky. "The heavens are sad." As his eyes moistened, ours did, too. We promised to return.

Vira Vira. East of Vira Vira, as far as the eye can see looking down the Huabayacu toward the Huallaga, hundreds of square miles of montaña *await scientific exploration.*

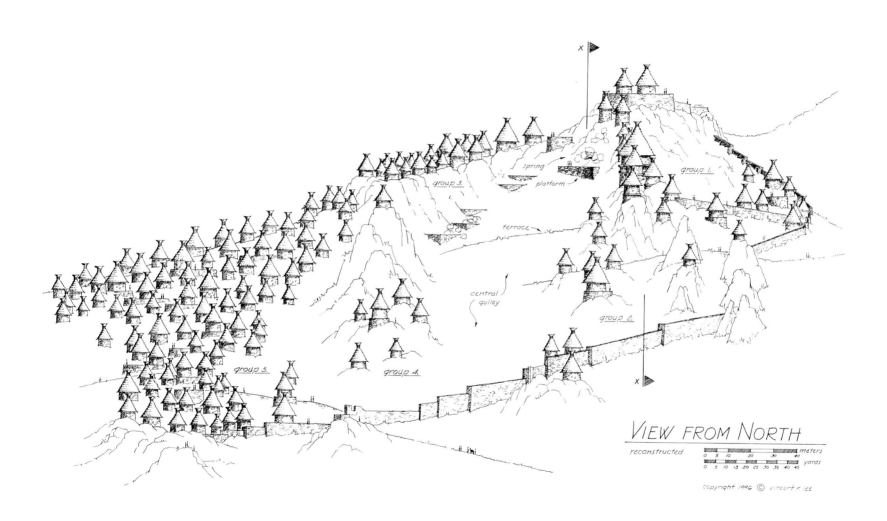

group 1.

group 3.

spring

platform

terrace

central gulley

group 2.

group 4.

group 5.

VIEW FROM NORTH

reconstructed

	meters
0 5 10 20 30 40	
0 5 10 15 20 25 30 35 40 45	yards

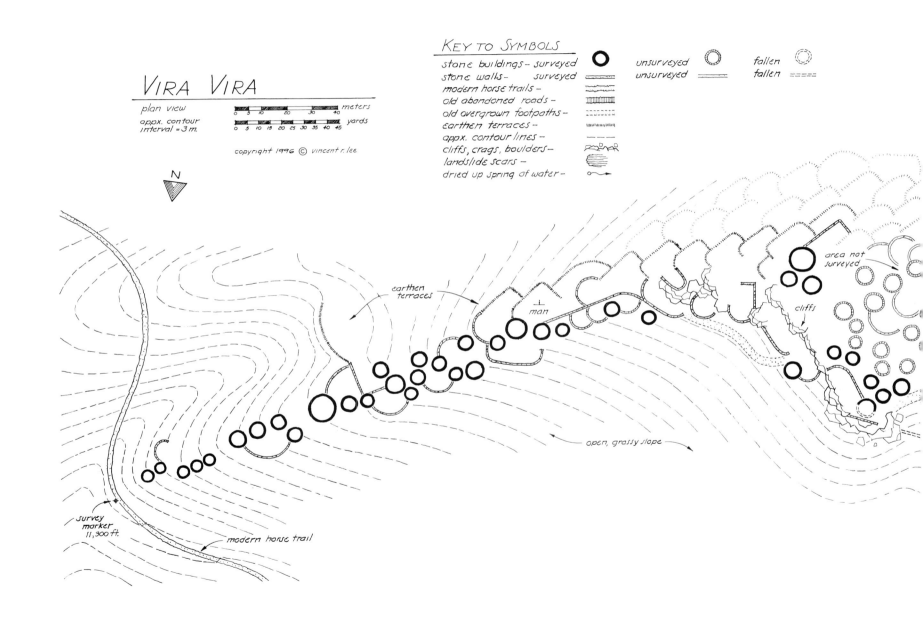

VIRA VIRA

plan view

appx. contour
interval = 3 m.

0 5 10 20 30 40 meters
0 5 10 15 20 25 30 35 40 45 yards

copyright 1996 © vincent r. lee

N

KEY TO SYMBOLS

stone buildings - surveyed · unsurveyed · fallen
stone walls - surveyed · unsurveyed · fallen
modern horse trails -
old abandoned roads -
old overgrown footpaths -
earthen terraces -
appx. contour lines -
cliffs, crags, boulders -
landslide scars -
dried up spring of water -

earthen
terraces

man

area not
surveyed

cliffs

open, grassy slope

survey
marker
11,300 ft.

modern horse trail

114

earthen terraces

area not surveyed

cliffs

cliffs

peak —
12,093 ft.

spring

platform

⊥ man

terraces

central
gulley

wall

gate

road

craqs

⊥ man

road

X ▶

X ▶

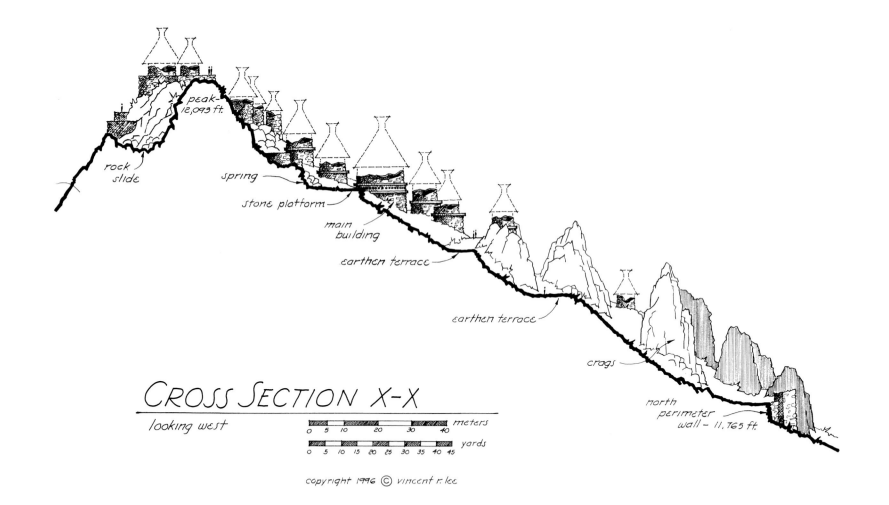

rock
slide

peak-
12,093 ft.

spring

stone platform

main
building

earthen terrace

earthen terrace

crags

north
perimeter
wall - 11,765 ft.

CROSS SECTION X-X

looking west

0 5 10 20 30 40 meters

0 5 10 15 20 25 30 35 40 45 yards

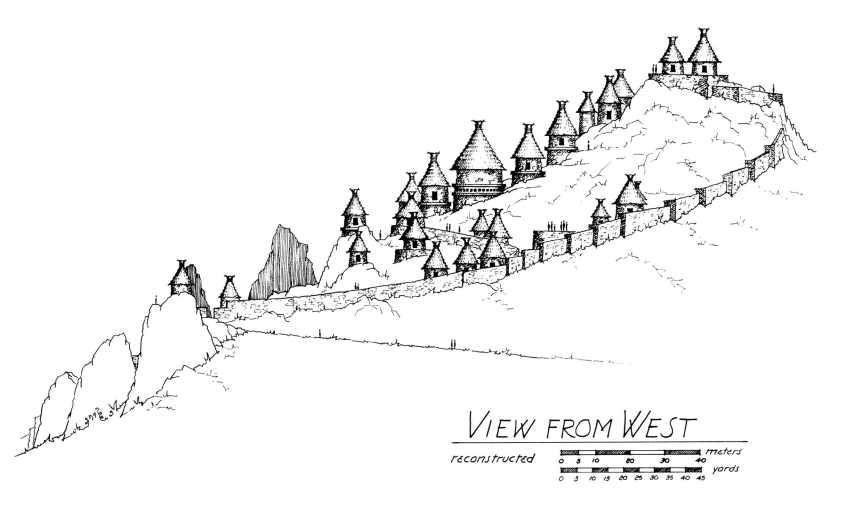

VIEW FROM WEST

reconstructed

					meters
0	5	10	20	30	40

								yards
0	5	10	15	20	25	30	35	40	45

copyright 1996 © vincent r. lee

117

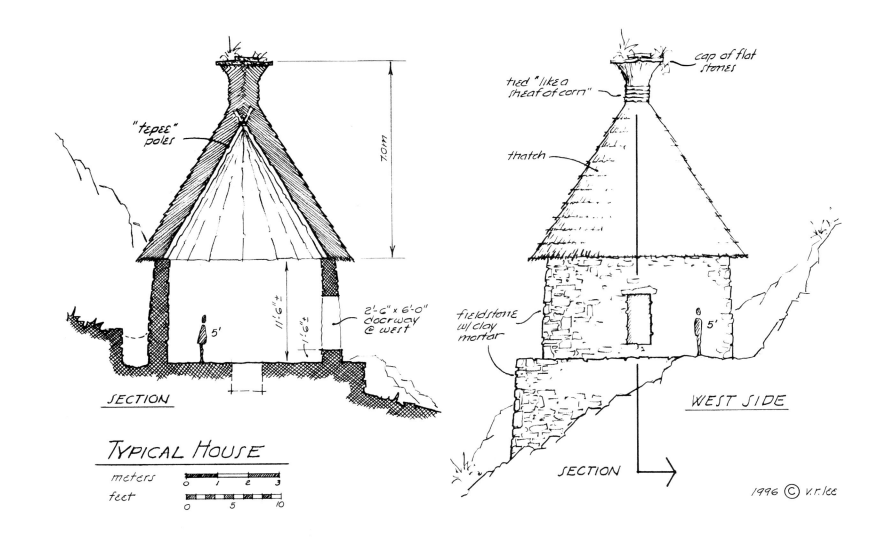

"tepee" poles

7.0 m

11'-6"±

1'-6"±

2'-6" x 6'-0" doorway @ west

SECTION

cap of flat stones

tied "like a sheaf of corn"

thatch

fieldstone w/ clay mortar

5'

WEST SIDE

SECTION

1996 © v.r. lee

TYPICAL HOUSE

meters
0 1 2 3

feet
0 5 10

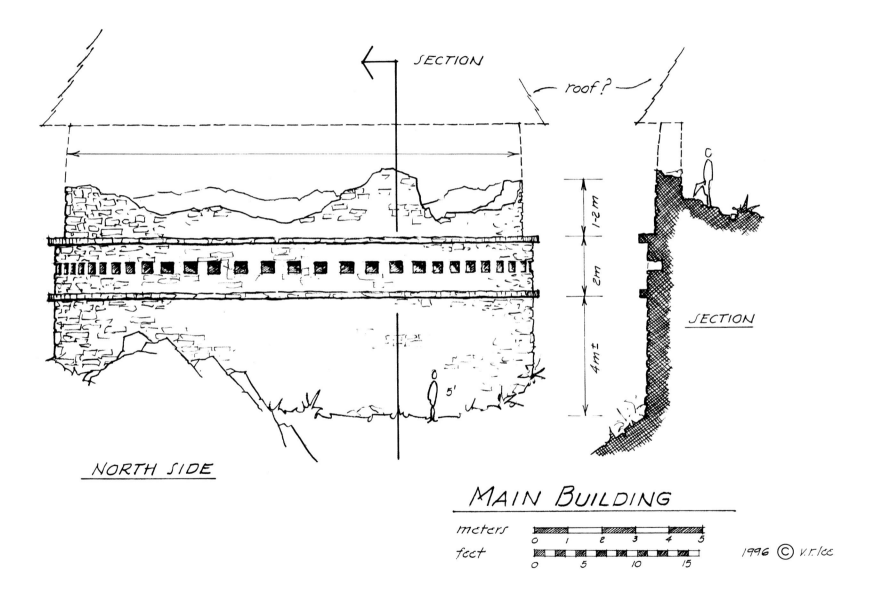

SECTION

roof?

1-2 m

2m

4m±

SECTION

5'

NORTH SIDE

MAIN BUILDING

meters
0 1 2 3 4 5

feet
0 5 10 15

1996 © v.r.lee

119

CHAPTER EIGHT

Epilogue: The Laguna de los Cóndores

Late in 1996 at the Laguna de los Cóndores (Lake of the Condors), approximately ten miles north–northeast of the Laguna Huayabamba, ranch hands clearing land for cattle grazing noticed a building perched in the steep, cloud–forested limestone cliffs that rise from the water's edge. They cut a trail to the site and made one of the most remarkable discoveries in Chachapoya archaeology. On a dry, sheltered ledge overlooking the lake they found a row of *chullpas*—plastered and painted masonry tombs. Inside the *chullpas* were over two hundred egg-shaped bundles containing mummified human remains wrapped in textiles and bound with knotted cords. Many had schematic faces embroidered on them. Around and above the *chullpas* was a wooden scaffolding, partially collapsed, that supported balconies on which were set additional mummies, several inside coffins made of wooden slats. Throughout the site were abundant and astonishingly well preserved funerary offerings: pottery, textiles, leather, feather work, netting, basketry, carved bone, shell and wood, pyro-engraved gourds, beads, ornaments of bronze, silver and gold, and several intact *khipu*. The tombs' discoverers immediately ransacked them, hacking open the mummy bundles in a feverish search for precious metal. In the process they irreparably damaged a unique scientific treasury.

Fortunately, the sale of artifacts plundered from the tombs came to the attention of police and archaeological authorities in April of 1997. Peter Lerche inventoried the site, which lies within his jurisdiction as an officer of the Instituto Nacional de Cultura. He was followed shortly thereafter by influential Amazonian archaeologist Federico Kauffmann Doig, as well as journalists and television crews. International attention was drawn to the mummies and their location was widely publicized. Within days a cottage industry sprang up, with local inhabitants guiding adventurous outsiders along the difficult trail across the bleak *cordillera* that separates the Laguna de los Cóndores from the nearest town, Leimebamba. Unsupervised, and in some cases unscrupulous, visitors trampled the debris left by the *huaqueros* and pilfered portable artifacts.

In July 1997, thanks to the efforts of archaeological writer Adriana von Hagen and physical anthropologist Sonia Guillén, the Laguna de los Cóndores was legally declared a *zona en emergencia*, off-

120

Laguna de los Cóndores. A row of chullpas protected by a rocky overhang.
A superstructure supports a coffin made of wooden slats.

Laguna de los Cóndores. An embroidered face animates a textile bundle containing
mummified human remains.

Laguna de los Cóndores. The planking of a wooden balcony projects from a shelf above representations of mythical creatures. As at other cliff tomb sites on the eastern flanks of the Central Cordillera, rock art abounds. Some of the rock art antedates the construction of the chullpas and was covered by them.

Laguna de los Cóndores. An Inka khipu, ignored by the huaqueros, lies draped across the remains of one of the mummy bundles which were removed from the chullpas. Several khipu were found at this site and in other, previously looted tombs nearby. Few khipu have ever been found in situ.

limits to all but authorized researchers. Adriana and Sonia also secured permission to salvage the mummies and excavate the *chullpas*, with financial assistance from The Discovery Channel. It was my good fortune to be invited by Adriana to accompany her to reconnoiter the site in preparation for the arrival of Sonia and the "dirt archaeologists."

As of this writing, analysis of the Laguna de los Cóndores material is still in process. It will be many months, possibly years, before definitive results will be available. However, preliminary indications are that the site, though disturbed, is of extraordinary archeological value. The *chullpas*, which are quintessentially Chachapoya in their architecture and therefore presumably pre-Inka, are built over earlier remains, as evidenced by pictographs that were obscured by their construction. The ceramics include colorfully decorated pots that are immediately recognizable as Inka, as well as Chimú, Cajamarca, and Chachapoya forms. Many of the ceramics seem to be hybrids, combining elements of these differing styles, and the textiles also blend Inka and Chachapoya designs. One glazed vessel is definitely of European-colonial era manufacture, although fundamentally Chimú in shape. This vessel, along with a few glass beads and a Christian cross, raise unanswered questions about how local populations were able to continue to leave offerings at the tombs without inviting looting and destruction by the Spanish.

Aside from the damage inflicted by the *huaqueros*, the mummies are extremely well-preserved—eloquent testimony to the skill of their pre-Columbian embalmers. The more elaborate mummies, some of which were lodged on the balconies above the *chullpas*, were perhaps Inka administrators and leaders of their *mitmaqkuna* (relocated populations). The bundled occupants of the *chullpas*, most of whom were probably Chachapoya, were apparently grouped (in some cases literally tied together) according to their *ayllu*, or clan. Across the lake from the tombs the ruins of a Chachapoya village, quite similar to Vira Vira, have been found. It is probably safe to assume that many of the people whose mummies were stored in the *chullpas* were the inhabitants of that settlement.

The discoveries at the Laguna de los Cóndores provide new and compelling evidence of the rich legacy of the ancient Chachapoya and move them closer to the prominence they deserve in the study of indigenous Andean civilization.

A Chachapoya Bibliography

Compiled with the generous assistance of Douglas Sharon

Alayza, J. 1892–93. Expedición Organizada por el Señor Alayza, Prefecto de Amazonas, á Indicación de la Sociedad Geográfica de Lima, para hacer Nuevos Estudios de la Fortaleza de Cuelap. Informe de la Comisión. *Boletín de la Sociedad Geográfica de Lima* 2:4–6: 153–160.

Alvarado, A. 1965/1555. Primeros descubrimientos y conquistas de los Chachapoyas por el Capitán Alonso de Alvarado. Memorias de las cosas primeras que acontecieron en los Chachapoyas. In *Relaciones Geográficas de Indias*. M. Jiménez de la Espada, ed. 3: 158–164: 164–168. Madrid: Biblioteca de Autores Españoles.

Amat Alazabal, H. 1978. Los Yaros: Destructores del Imperio Wari. *III Congreso Peruano del Hombre y la Cultura Andina*. R. Matos, ed. 2: 614–640.

Anonymous. 1985. Fortifications and Temples Found at Gran Vilaya Site. *Lima Times* 544: 1–2.

Anonymous. 1985. Gran Vilaya. *South American Explorer* 12: 24–26, 45.

Bandelier, A. 1940/1907. Los Indios y las ruinas aborígenas cerca de Chachapoyas en el norte del Perú. *Chaski* 1:2: 13–59.

Basadre, M. 1891–92. Torre de Babel en el Perú. *Boletín de la Sociedad Geográfica de Lima* 1: 10–12: 440–448.

Betanzos, J. 1996/1576. *Narrative of the Incas*. Austin: University of Texas Press.

Bonavía, D. 1968. *Las ruinas del Abiseo*. Lima: Universidad Peruana de Ciencias y Tecnología.

Bonavía, D. 1990. Les ruines de l'Abiseo. In *Inca Perou: 3,000 ans d'histoire*, pp. 248–261. Brussels: Musées Royaux d'Art et d'Histoire.

Bower, B. 1985. A lost and found city in Peru gets new perspective. *Science News* 127:8: 117.

Brush, S. 1977. *Mountain, Field, and Family: The Economy and Human Ecology of an Andean Valley*. Philadelphia: University of Pennsylvania Press.

Cahill, T. 1977. Cahill among the Ruins in Peru. *Outside* December 1977: 35–42, 72–77, 79–80. Reprinted in *Jaguars Ripped My Flesh*, pp. 63–88. New York: Bantam Books (1987).

Cahill, T. 1987. Bright Lights, Not-So-Lost Cities. *Outside* April 1987: 35–39.

Cavatrunci, C. 1983. I Chachapoya del Perú Settentrionale: Archeologia e Storia. In *Antisuyo, ultimo sogno Inca*, pp. 99–107. Venice: Mirano.

Church, W. 1991. La ocupación temprana del Gran Pajatén. *Revista del Museo de Arqueología* 2: 7–38. Trujillo.

Church, W. 1993. *Evidence for Prehistoric Highland-Tropical Forest Interaction from Manachaqui Cave in the Northeastern Highlands of Peru: Preliminary Report*. Paper presented at the Society for American Archaeology meeting. St. Louis, MO.

Church, W. 1994. Early Occupations of Gran Pajatén, Peru. *Andean Past* 4: 281–318.

Church, W. 1996. *Prehistoric Cultural Development and Interregional Interaction in the Tropical Montane Forests of Peru*. Doctoral dissertation. Yale University.

Cieza de Leon, P. 1959/1553. *The Incas*. H. de Onis, trans. V. W. von Hagen, ed. Norman: University of Oklahoma Press.

Cieza de Leon, P. 1986/1554. *Crónica del Perú*. Lima: Pontificia Universidad Católica del Perú.

Corbero Valdivia, H. 1987. Estudio del Suelo y Delimitación del Area de Protección y Reserva del Complejo Arqueológico de Kuelap. MS. Chachapoyas: INC Amazonas.

Crisóstomo Nieto, J. 1905/1843. Nota del Juez Nieto al Prefecto de Amazonas. In *Colección de leyes, decretos, resoluciones i otros documentos oficiales referentes al Departamento de Loreto*. C. Larrabure i Correa 6: 446–450. Lima: Imp. de la Opinión Nacional.

Cundy, R. 1969. Abiceo—link with Pre-Columbian Peru. *Geographical Magazine* 41:12: 883–891.

Curtis, J. 1980. Uchucmarca, pueblo de misterios en los Andes peruanos. *Geo Mundo* (July).

Davis, M. 1985a. *Chachapoyas: The Cloud People: An Anthropological Survey*. Monetville, Ontario, Canada: Self-published.

Davis, M. 1985b. *Chachapoyas: The Cloud People: Additions, Corrections, and Selected Themes*. Monetville, Ontario, Canada: Self-published.

Davis, M. 1989. *The Casa Redonda in La Jalca Grande*. Noëlville, Ontario, Canada: Self-published.

Davis, M. 1993. *Yurak Urko*. Noëlville, Ontario, Canada: Self-published. [Morgan Davis's works may be purchased directly from him via General Delivery, Noëlville, Ontario POM 2NO, Canada.]

Deza Rivasplata, J. 1975–76. "La Playa" Un complejo arqueológico en la cuenca del Abiseo.

Arqueología, PUC: Boletín del Seminario de Arqueología 17–18: 43–50, plus six unnumbered plates (Publicación no. 106 del Instituto Riva-Agüero). Lima: Pontificia Universidad Católica del Perú.

Dyott, G., 1922. *Silent Highways of the Jungle*, pp. 50-85. New York: G. P. Putnam's Sons.

Espinoza Soriano, W. 1967. Los señoríos étnicos de Chachapoyas y la alianza hispano-chacha. *Revista Histórica* 30: 224–333.

Espinoza Soriano, W. 1978. Los Chachapoyas y Cañares de Chiara (Huamanga), Aliados de España. *Historia, Problema y Promesa* 1. Lima: Pontificia Universidad Católica del Perú.

Espinoza, V. 1948/1626. *Compendio y descripción de las Indias Occidentales*. Washington, DC: Smithsonian Institution.

Flornoy, B. 1943. Trabajos de la Misión Francesa del Amazonas en la región de Angulo. *Boletín de la Sociedad Geográfica de Lima* 60: 20–25.

Flornoy, B. 1946. *Amazone Terres et hommes, Découverte des sources*. Paris: Cercle du Bibliophile.

Garcilaso de la Vega, Inca. 1966/1609. *Royal Commentaries of the Incas and General History of Peru, Part 1*. Translation by H. Livermore. Austin: University of Texas Press.

Gates, C. 1960s and 1970s. Numerous articles relating to Chachapoya ruins in his weekly newspaper *Voz de Amazonas*. Chachapoyas, Peru.

Gil, N. 1936. Las Tumbas Estructurales de Aispachaka. *Boletín de la Sociedad Geográfica de Lima* 53:4, 235–239.

Gil, N. 1938. Dos Pueblos Prehistóricos Kuelapenses: Kacta y Chipuric. *Boletín de la Sociedad Geográfica de Lima* 55:2–3, 132–139.

Gilbert, S. 1985. Lost Cities of the Andes: An Explorer Restakes His Jungle Claims. *Science Digest* (June), pp. 46–53, 83.

Harth-Terré, E. 1968. Pajatén, arqueología del Utcubamba. *El arquitecto peruano* 347–348: 41–50.

Hemming, J. 1970. *The Conquest of the Incas*. New York: Harcourt Brace.

Herrera, J. 1922. Tragica Exploración al Huayabamba de los Hermanos Seljan (15 de octubre de 1912 al 30 de abril de 1913). *Boletín de la Sociedad Geográfica de Lima* 39: 52–62.

Horkheimer, H. 1959. Algunas Consideraciones de la arqueología en el Valle del Utcubamba. *Actas y Trabajos del II Congreso Nacional de Historia del Perú* 2: 71–95.

Instituto Geográfico Nacional (IGN, formerly Instituto Geográfico Militar). 1968–72. *Carta Nacional, 1:100,000.*

IGN. 1973. *Republica del Perú. Mapa Físico Político, 1:1,000,000.*

IGN. 1981. *Departamento de Amazonas. Mapa Físico Político, 1:600,000.*

IGN. 1984. *Mapa Planimétrico de Imágenes de Satélite, 1:250,000.*

IGN. 1985. *Departamento de San Martín. Mapa Físico Político, 1:500,000.*

Izaguirre, B. 1922. *Historia de las misiones franciscanas*. Lima: Talleres Tipográficas de la Penetenciaría. [Includes an early photograph of a decorated Chachapoya building.]

Kauffmann Doig, F. 1980. "Los Pinchudos": Exploración de Ruinas intactas en la Selva. *Boletín de Lima* 7: 26–31.

Kauffmann Doig, F. 1983a. L'Antisuyo del Nord (risultati di due spedizioni). In *Antisuyo, ultimo sogno Inca*, pp. 75–98. Venice: Mirano.

Kauffmann Doig, F. 1983b. Expresiones culturales en la Sierra. In *Manual de Arqueología Peruana*, pp. 525–534. Lima: Ediciones PEISA.

Kauffmann Doig, F. 1984a. Pucullo y figuras antropomorfos de madera en el antisuyo. *Cielo Abierto* 29: 46–52.

Kauffmann Doig, F. 1984b. Sarcófagos Antropomorfos en el Alto Amazonas (Informe Preliminar). *Boletín de Lima* 6:35, 46–48.

Kauffmann Doig, F. 1986. Sarcófagos Pre-Incas en los Andes Amazónicos Peruanos. *Kuntur* 1:4–9.

Kauffmann Doig, F. 1987. *Andes Amazónicos: Investigaciones Arqueológicas 1980–1986 (Expediciones Antisuyo)*. Lima: Banco Continental.

Kauffmann Doig, F. 1989a. Andes Amazónicos, sitios intervenidos por la expedición Antisuyo/86. *Arqueológicas* 20: 5–57.

Kauffmann Doig, F. 1989b. *Investigaciones arqueológicas en los Andes Amazónicos 1980–1988*. Lima: Instituto de Arqueología Amazónica.

Kauffmann Doig, F. 1993a. Le Ande Amazzoniche. *Peru, atto primo*, pp. 455–534. Venice: Erizzo Editrice.

Kauffmann Doig, F. 1993b. *Los Andes Amazónicos en el Proceso Cultural Andino*. Lima: Instituto de Arqueología Amazónica.

Kauffmann Doig, F., and G. Ligabue. 1990. Les Andes Amazoniennes. In *Inca Perou: 3,000 ans d'histoire*, pp. 262–275. Brussels: Musées Royaux d'Art et d'Histoire.

Kieffer, P. 1910. *Excursión a Cuelap (Departamento de Amazonas, Perú)*. E. Rosay, ed. Lima: Librería Francesa Científica.

Langlois, L. 1933. Ultimas exploraciones en el Perú. *Revista del Museo Nacional* 2:2: 126–128.

Langlois, L. 1934. Las ruinas de Cuelap. *Boletín de la Sociedad Geográfica de Lima* 51:1: 20–34.

Langlois, L. 1939–40. Utcubamba. Investigaciones arqueológicas en este valle del departamento de Amazonas, Perú. *Revista del Museo Nacional* 8:2: 224–249 (1939); 9:1: 33–72 (1940); 9:2: 191–228 (1940).

Langlois, L. 1948. Recherches archéologiques dans la Province des Chachapoyas (Perou septentrional). *26th International Congress of Americanists, Proceedings* (Seville, 1935) 1: 153–167. Madrid.

Lennon, T., Church, W., and Cornejo, M. 1985. *Reporte Preliminar de los trabajos realizados por el Proyecto de Investigación en el Parque Nacional Río Abiseo*. Boulder: Río Abiseo National Park Research Project, University of Colorado.

Lennon, T., Church, W., and Cornejo, M. 1986. *Informe Final 1985: Investigaciones sobre los recursos culturales del Parque Nacional Río Abiseo*. Boulder: Río Abiseo National Park Research Project, University of Colorado.

Lennon, T., Church, W., and Cornejo, M. 1987. *Informe Final 1986: Investigaciones sobre los recursos culturales en el Parque Nacional Río Abiseo*. Boulder: Río Abiseo National Park Research Project, University of Colorado.

Lennon, T., Church, W., and Cornejo, M. 1989. Investigaciones arqueológicas en el Parque Nacional Río Abiseo, San Martín. *Boletín de Lima* 62: 43–56.

Leo, M., and Ortiz, E. 1982. Un Parque Nacional "Gran Pajatén." *Boletín de Lima* 22: 47–60.

Lerche, P. 1986. *Häuptlingstum Jalca: Bevölkerung und Ressourcen bei den vorspanischen Chachapoya; Peru*. Berlin: Dietrich Reimer Verlag.

Lerche, P. 1995. *Los Chachapoya y los Símbolos de su Historia*. Lima: Servicios Editoriales César Gayoso.

Lerche, P. 1996. *Chachapoyas, Guía de viajeros*. Lima: Intigráfica César Gayoso.

Ludeña, H. n.d. (circa 1992). *Manuscritos Sobre Chachapoyas en Varios Archivos Siglos XVI–XIX*. MS. Boulder: Río Abiseo National Park Research Project, University of Colorado.

McGraw, J., Oncina, M., Sharon, D., and Torres Más, C. 1996. *Kuélap: A Solar Observatory?* San Diego Museum of Man, *Ethnic Technology Notes* No. 24. San Diego, CA..

Middendorf, E. 1895. *Peru, 3: Das Hochland von Peru*. Berlin: Robert Oppenheim (Gustav Schmidt).

Mogrovejo, T. 1921/1539. Libro de Visitas. *Revista del Archivo Nacional de Perú* 2:1: 66–68.

Muscutt, K. 1987. A Trophy Head Pictograph from the Peruvian Amazon. In *Rock Art Papers* 5. K. Hedges, ed., *San Diego Museum Papers* 23: 155–160.

Muscutt, K. 1989. Cueva de Osiris: A Pictograph Site in the Peruvian Amazon. In *Rock Art Papers* 6. K. Hedges, ed., *San Diego Museum Papers* 24: 107–110.

Muscutt, K., Lee, V., and Sharon, D. 1993. *Vira Vira: A "New" Chachapoyas Site*. Wilson, WY: Sixpac Manco Publications. [Sixpac Manco Publications, P.O. Box 107, Wilson, WY 83014, publishes Andean monographs by Vince Lee.]

Muscutt, K., Lee, V., and Sharon, D. 1994. Vira Vira: A "New" Chachapoyas Site. *South American Explorer* 39: 5–30.

Muscutt, K., Lee, V., and Sharon, D. 1996. Vira Vira, un nuevo sitio Chachapoya. *Kuelap, Boletín Cultural* 110. Chachapoyas: INC Amazonas.

Narváez, A. 1986. Rasgos arquitectónicos de la Fortaleza de Kuelap. *Kuelap, Boletín Cultural* 66. Chachapoyas: INC Amazonas.

Narváez, A. 1988. Kuelap: Una ciudad fortificada en los Andes nor-orientales de Amazonas, Perú. In *Arquitectura y Arqueología*. V. Rangel, ed., 13–16: 8: 115–142. Chiclayo.

Narváez, A. 1996. La fortaleza de Kuélap. *Arkinka*, Año 1, No. 12, November: 92–108.

Nestarez, F. 1929. *Cuentos, Tradiciones, Leyendas y Costumbres Quechuas*. Lima: Talleres Gráficos de la Penitenciaria.

Pagador, M. 1872. *Floresta Española-Americana* 1: 356–360. Lima: Imprenta del Estado.

Paz Soldán, M. 1862. *Geografía del Perú* 1: 172–173. Paris: Fermin Didot.

Pérez Alvarado, E. 1938. Arqueología de Amazonas 1. (Various articles, transcripts of propaganda broadcasts, with maps.) *Momento Cultural* 1–6. Ministerio de Guerra.

Pia, E. 1993. Untitled account of 1988 excavations at Kuelap. *Kuelap, Boletín Cultural* 101. Chachapoyas: INC Amazonas.

Pimentel, V. 1967. Pajatén. *Fenix: Revista de la Biblioteca Nacional* 17: 34–45. Lima.

Pimentel, V. 1969. Pajatén. *Cultura y Pueblo* 15–16: 10–13.

Poindexter, M. 1930. *The Ayar-Incas* 1: 110–121. New York: Horace Liveright.

Raimondi, A. 1874. *El Perú*, Tomo 1: 147–158, 409–414. Lima: Imprenta del Estado.

Raimondi, A. n.d. (circa 1900). *Mapa del Perú, 1:500,000: Foja 12*. Paris.

Raimondi, A. 1905/1862. Informe sobre la provincia litoral de Loreto por don Antonio Raimondi. In *Colección de leyes, decretos, resoluciones i otros documentos oficiales referentes al Departamento de Loreto*. C. Larrabure i Correa 7: 118–183. Lima: Imp. de la Opinión Nacional.

Raimondi, A. 1942–43, 1855, 1857–61. *Notas de Viajes para su obra "El Perú"* 1: 408–422; 2: 20–35. Lima. Imprenta Torres Aguirre.

Rangel i Fayas. 1905/1827. Descripción de la diócesis de Mainas é historia del gobierno de su primer obispo, Rangel i Fayas, descripción por este mismo para ser presentada á S. M. el rei de España. In *Colección de leyes, decretos, resoluciones i otros documentos oficiales referentes al Departamento de Loreto*. C. Larrabure i Correa 8: 314–315, 329–330. Lima: Imp. de la Opinión Nacional.

Ravines, R. 1972. Los caciques de Pausamarca: algo más sobre las étnias de Chachapoyas. *Historia y Cultura* 6: 217–247.

Ravines, R. 1978. Antiguos sitios de ocupación en el Río Huayabamba, Perú. *Historia, Problema y Promesa. Homenaje a Jorge Basadre* 1: 521–532. Lima.

Ravines, R. 1982a. *Panorama de la arqueología andina*. Lima: IEP.

Ravines, R. 1982b. Yacimientos Arqueológicos de la región nororiental del Perú. *Amazonia Peruana* 4:7: 139–175.

Reichlen, H., and Reichlen, P. 1950. Recherches archéologiques dans les Andes du haut Utcubamba. *Journal de la Société des Américanistes, Nouvelle série* 34: 219–250.

Rocha, A. The Other Cuzco/El Otro Cusco. *Peru El Dorado*, 8: 56–64, Lima.

Rojas Ponce, P. 1966. Un informe sobre las ruinas de Pajatén. *Cuadernos Americanos* (septiembre–octubre), pp. 119–127.

Rojas Ponce, P. 1967. The Ruins of Pajatén. (Translation by D. Lathrap.) *Archaeology* 20:1: 9–17.

Ruiz, A. 1969. Alfarería del estilo Huari en Kuelap. *PUC: Boletín del Seminario de Arqueología* 4: 60–65.

Ruiz Estrada, A. 1972. *La alfarería de Cuelap: Tradición y cambio*. Tesis de Bachiller. Lima: Universidad Nacional Mayor de San Marcos.

Ruiz Estrada, A. 1977. Los monumentos arqueológicos de Tuich (Departamento de Amazonas). *Investigaciones Arqueológicas* 1. Lima

Ruiz Estrada, A. 1985. Los Monumentos Arqueológicos de Leimebamba. *Boletín de Lima* 7:42: 69–82.

Ruiz Estrada, A. 1994. La Cirugía Prehispánica en el Departamento de Amazonas, Perú. *Sequillao* 3:7: 149–170.

Ruiz Estrada, A. n.d. *Pumachaca: Una Litoescultura en el Valle del Utcubamba*. Huacho: Universidad Nacional José Faustino Sanchez Carrión.

Salz, J. 1995. City of the Clouds. *Escape* (Winter), pp. 38–45. [Adventure-travelogue of a visit to Vira Vira.]

Sarmiento de Gamboa, P. 1960/1572. *Historia Indica*, pp. 193–279. Madrid: Biblioteca de Autores Españoles 135, Ediciones Atlas.

Savoy, G. 1965–70. Various articles. *Andean Airmail and Peruvian Times*, Vol. 25, no. 1294; Vol. 26, no. 1331; Vol. 26, no. 1344; Vol. 26, no. 1346; Vol. 26, no. 1357; Vol. 27, no. 1326;

Vol. 27, no. 1401; Vol. 27, no. 1403; Vol. 27, no. 1408; Vol. 28, no. 1431; Vol. 28, no. 1435; Vol. 28, no. 1455; Vol. 28, no. 1461; Vol. 29, no. 1465; Vol. 29, no. 1494; and July 30 and Aug. 21, 1970. Lima.

Savoy, G. 1970. *Antisuyo: The Search for the Lost Cities of the Andes.* New York: Simon & Schuster.

Savoy, G. 1997. Jungle Explorer. An Interview with Gene Savoy. *The Lima Times*: Vol. 22, no. 3, pp. 10–13, 39.

Schjellerup, I. 1979. Problems in the Ethnohistory of Uchucmarca. *42nd International Congress of Americanists Proceedings* (Paris, 1976) 9: 221–231. Paris.

Schjellerup, I. 1980. Documents on Paper and in Stone. A preliminary report on the Inca ruins in Cochabamba, Province of Chachapoyas, Peru. *Folk* 22/23: 299–311.

Schjellerup, I. 1984. Cochabamba—An incaic administrative centre in the rebellious province of Chachapoyas. In BAR Internaćional Series 210, *Current Archaeological Projects in the Central Andes.* A. Kendall, ed., pp. 161–187. 44th International Congress of Americanists. Manchester, 1982.

Schjellerup, I. 1985. Observations on ridged fields and terracing systems in the northern highlands of Peru. *Tools and Tillage* 5:2: 100–121.

Schjellerup, I. 1986. Ploughing in Chuquibamba, Peru. *Tools and Tillage* 5:3: 180–189.

Schjellerup, I. 1987. Gift Exchange Ceremonies in the Northern Highlands of Peru. *Folk* 29: 43–53.

Schjellerup, I. 1989. *Children of the Stones. Hijos de las piedras.* Royal Danish Academy of Sciences and Letters, Commission for Research on the History of Agricultural Implements and Field Structures 7. Copenhagen.

Schjellerup, I. 1990. Recherches archéologiques et historiques au Chachapoyas—Perou. In *Inca Perou: 3,000 ans d'histoire,* pp. 236–247. Brussels: Musées Royaux d'Art et d'Histoire.

Schjellerup, I. 1992a. La agricultura prehispánica en el territorio de la Provincia de Chachapoyas, Departamento de Amazonas, Perú. *Revista del Museo de Arqueología* 3: 142–157. Trujillo.

Schjellerup, I. 1992b. Patrones de asentamiento en las faldas orientales de los Andes de la región de Chachapoyas. In *Estudios de Arqueología Peruana.* D. Bonavía, ed., pp. 355–373. Lima: FOMCIENCIAS.

Schjellerup, I. 1997. *Incas and Spaniards in the Conquest of the Chachapoyas, Archaeological and Ethnohistorical Research in the North-eastern Andes of Peru.* GOTARC, series B, Gothenburg Archeological Theses, 7. Götebotg University.

Schjellerup, I., Jakobsen, J., Jorgensen, J., and Jorgensen, L. 1986–87. Cazadores de cabezas en sitios pre-Inca de Chachapoyas, Amazonas. *Revista del Museo Nacional* 48: 139–85.

Schjellerup, I., and Sorensen, A. M. 1992. *Bishopken, antropologen og botanikeren—nutid moder fortid i Andesbjergene.* Copenhagen: Laegefoeningens Forlag. [Eighteenth-century Bishop Martinez de Compañon's itinerary, reports, and drawings.]

Senèze, P. 1877. Perforations crâniennes sur d'anciens crânes du haut Pérou. *Société d'Anthropologie de Paris, Bulletin 2ᵉ*: 12: 561–563.

Senèze, P., and Noetzli, J. 1877. Sur les momies découvertes dans le haut Pérou. *Société d'Anthropologie de Paris, Bulletin 2ᵉ*: 12: 640–641.

Senèze, P., and Noetzli, J. 1885. Voyage dans les Républiques de l'Equateur et du Pérou. *Société de Géographie, Bulletin 7ᵉ*: 6: 523–593.

Tibesar, A. 1953. *Franciscan Beginnings in Colonial Peru,* pp. 58–61. Washington, DC: Academy of American Franciscan History.

Thompson, D. 1973a. Archaeological Investigations in the Eastern Andes of Northern Peru. *40th International Congress of Americanists, Proceedings* (1972) 1: 363–369. Rome–Genoa.

Thompson, D. 1973b. Investigaciones arqueológicas en los Andes orientales del norte del Perú. *Revista del Museo Nacional* 39: 117–125. Lima.

Thompson, D. 1976. Prehistory of the Uchucmarca Valley in the North Highlands of Peru. *41st International Congress of Americanists, Proceedings* (1974) 2: 99–106. Mexico City.

Thompson, D. 1984. Ancient Highland Connections with Selva and Coast: Evidence from Uchucmarca, Peru. In BAR International Series 194: *Social and Economic Organization in the Prehispanic Andes.* D. Browman, R. Burger, M. Rivera, eds., pp. 73–78.

Tomkievicz, S. 1967. The Lost City of Pajaten. *Horizon* 9:4: 62–67.

Unanue, H., and Sobreviela, M. 1963. *Historia de las misiones de Caxamarquilla.* Madrid: Bibliotheca Tenanitla 6. [Late eighteenth-century missionary activities. Sobreviela's 1790 map of the Huallaga and environs is reproduced in Herndon, *Exploration of the Amazon,* 1853.]

Vaughan, D. 1986. Lost and Found. *South American Explorer* 13: 4–21.

Vega Ocampo, A. 1970. *El Complejo Pirca Pirca (Provincia de Bolívar), Novedad é Importancia de sus Patrones de Arquitectura y Cerámica en la Arqueología Liberteña.* Tesis. Universidad Nacional de Trujillo.

Vega Ocampo, A. 1977. El Complejo Arqueológico de Uchucmarca, Trabajo de Investigación: El Conjunto de "Pirca Pirca." *Revista Universitaria* 30. Trujillo.

Vega Ocampo, A. 1978. Complejo Arqueológico de Uchucmarca: Descripción del Elemento Cerámica de Pirca-Pirca. *Investigación Arqueológica* 2: 8–19. Trujillo.

Vega Ocampo, A. 1979. *Importancia Arqueológica de la Provincia de Bolívar.* Trujillo: Universidad Nacional de Trujillo.

Vega Ocampo, A. 1982. Complejo Arqueológico de Uchucmarca, Conjunto Pirca Pirca; Sus Cámaras Internas. *Investigación Arqueológica* 4: 41–45. Trujillo.

von Hagen, A. and Guillén, S. 1997. Tombs with a view. *Archaeology* 51 (2): 48–54.

von Hagen, V. W. 1957. *Highway of the Sun.* New York: Duell, Sloan and Pearce.

von Hagen, V. W. 1954. Al terminar sus tareas, la Expedición Von Hagen descubre una antigua ciudad de piedra. *El Comercio,* 7 December : 3. Lima.

Weberbauer, A. 1920. La salida de Patás al Huallaga estudiada en la ruta de Pajatén. *Boletín de la Sociedad Geográfica de Lima* 36:1: 5–13.

Wertheman, A. 1892–93. Ruinas de la fortaleza de Cuelap. *Boletín de la Sociedad Geográfica de Lima* 2:4–6: 147–153.

Wheeler, K. 1994. Back of Beyond in Peru. In *New York Times Magazine,* part 2 (November 13).

Wheeler, K. 1996. Peruvian Gothic. *Outside,* November: 64–70, 158–63. Boulder, CO.

Wheeler, K. 1997. Road to Ruins. *Escape,* January: 56–63, 100–2. Santa Monica, CA.

Wiener, C. 1884. Amazone et Cordillères. In *Le Tour du monde* 48:2: 385–416. Paris.

Wood, R. 1967 El misterio de Pajatén. *Américas* 19:7: 7–16.

Xesspe, M. 1937. Historia de la Expedición arqueologica al Marañón en 1937. In *Arqueología del Valle de Casma.* J. Tello. Lima, 1956.

Young, K., Church, W., Leo, M., and Moore, P. 1994. Threats to Río Abiseo National Park, Northern Peru. *Ambio* 23:4–5: 312–314.

Zevallos Quiñones, J. 1966. Onomástica prehispánica de Chachapoyas. *Lenguaje y Ciencias* 20: 27–41.

Zevallos Quiñones, J. 1987. Introducción a la etnohistoria Chachapoyas. *Kuelap, Boletín Cultural.* Chachapoyas: INC Amazonas.

Zubiate Zabarburu, V. 1984. *Guía arqueológica del departamento de Amazonas.* Chachapoyas, Peru. [Pp. 30–32 reproduce the 1964 *Informe* of the rediscovery of Gran Pajatén.]